CONFESSING THE FAITH TODAY
A FRESH LOOK AT THE BELGIC CONFESSION

CONFESSING THE FAITH TODAY
A FRESH LOOK AT THE BELGIC CONFESSION

Allan J. Janssen

WIPF & STOCK · Eugene, Oregon

CONFESSING THE FAITH TODAY
A Fresh Look at the Belgic Confession

Copyright © 2016 Allan J. Janssen. All rights reserved. Except for brief quotations in critical publications or reviews, no part of this book may be reproduced in any manner without prior written permission from the publisher. Write: Permissions, Wipf and Stock Publishers, 199 W. 8th Ave., Suite 3, Eugene, OR 97401.

Wipf & Stock
An Imprint of Wipf and Stock Publishers
199 W. 8th Ave., Suite 3
Eugene, OR 97401

www.wipfandstock.com

PAPERBACK ISBN: 978-1-4982-8624-4
HARDCOVER ISBN: 978-1-4982-8626-8
EBOOK ISBN: 978-1-4982-8625-1

Manufactured in the U.S.A.   10/28/16

The Belgic Confession is reprinted with permission from *Our Faith*, © 2013 Faith Alive Christian Resources. Permission granted January 2016.

Scripture quotations are from the New Revised Standard Version Bible, copyright © 1989 by the Division of Christian Education of the National Council of Churches of Christ in the United States of America, and are used by permission. All rights reserved.

The poem "To Life!" by Micheal O'Siahail is reprinted by permission of Bloodaxe Books on behalf of the author.

Permission to reprint portions of "Our Song of Hope" is granted by Reformed Church Press, 475 Riverside Drive, New York, NY 10115. All rights reserved.

CONTENTS

PREFACE

THIS BOOK WAS GENERATED from a double need. The first and most obvious is that for the past fifteen plus years I have taught the so-called "Standards of Unity" to candidates for professional ministry in the Reformed Church in America. The Standards include sixteenth- and seventeenth-century documents—the Belgic Confession, the Heidelberg Catechism, and the Canons of Dort—as well as the recently adopted Belhar Confession. The challenge was and is to help future ministers comprehend how old confessions of faith might still not only engage believers in the early twenty first century, but might assist them as they confess the faith today. Moreover, the school at which I teach, New Brunswick Theological Seminary, is situated in a context distant from that of even a few decades ago, when most students were white males raised in Reformed churches. Students now come from diverse racial and cultural backgrounds, living and working in a society that is not only culturally diverse, but religiously so as well. Can the church confess a sixteenth-century document with integrity in twenty-first-century urban America?

The second need is more diffuse. To all appearances the old Standards have largely fallen into disuse in the church. This is less the case with the Heidelberg Catechism, still beloved by many in Reformed churches for its warm, personal tone.[1] But one hears little reference to the Belgic Confession (the only comprehensive confession properly understood) in ecclesiastical discussions. Most ministers willingly subscribe to the confession when they make their ministerial declaration upon ordination, but few engage it explicitly in practice. Is this because both the categories and vocabulary of the confession have become antiquated?

---

1. Although the use of the Heidelberg for catechetical instruction of the young also appears to have fallen into disuse in large sections of the church.

I suspect that that has, in fact, become the case, and for good reason. For Reformed churches, confessions are living documents, and so contemporary. The Word is living and active and so engages us in the time and places of our living. While the Word is the "same, yesterday and today and forever" (Heb 13:8), it meets us in ever new contexts, and so speaks to us what we need to hear, which comforts and challenges us in ever new ways. Hence, Reformed churches produce new confessions in ever-changing situations. As the Presbyterian Church (USA) puts it, ". . . the creeds and confessions of this church reflect a particular stance within the history of God's people."[2]

This has been the case with three Reformed churches in the United States. The Presbyterian Church (USA) added its "Confession of 1967" to its *Book of Confessions*, and more recently "A Brief Statement of Faith." In 2008 the Christian Reformed Church in North America adopted its "Our World Belongs to God" as a "contemporary witness." Already in the 1950s, the church I serve, the Reformed Church in America, began discussions of a contemporary confession, although with little result. In 1978 it did produce "Our Song of Hope." While that document did not achieve confessional status, it was adopted as a "statement of the church's faith for use in its ministry of witness, teaching, and worship."[3] More recently, in 2010, the Belhar Confession was adopted as a "doctrinal standard" in the church, although it was a confession received from the Uniting Reformed Church of Southern Africa.[4]

Nonetheless, the Belgic Confession remains the only comprehensive confession of faith in the Reformed Church in America (as well as the Christian Reformed Church).[5] So the question remains: does a sixteenth-century confession articulate the faith in a twenty-first-century context? This book is an attempt to answer that question, and it answers positively, if sometimes with hesitance. Each chapter includes a section entitled "Context" that sets the old confession within the context of the contemporary church and society.

2. *Book of Order*, G-2.0300, cited in Small, "Church's Conversation with the Confessions," 10.

3. *Acts of Proceedings of the 172nd Regular Session of the General Synod*, 37.

4. The confession was first adopted by the then Dutch Reformed Mission Church in South Africa (later to become URCSA) in 1986. For a discussion of the history and content of the Belhar Confession, see Naudé, *Neither Calendar nor Clock*.

5. The other standards are either not strictly confessions (the Heidelberg Catechism and the Canons of Dort) or not comprehensive (the Belhar Confession).

Even so, this work remains perspectival, as is the case for all writing. The author is a white male who has served middle-class Reformed churches for over forty years. As one who was born and raised in the Reformed Church in America, my theological formation has been in that tradition. That perspective shapes my own understanding of the context in which the confession may find traction. That context shifts as one enters other "worlds" where God meets God's communion of saints. The reader is invited to engage in a living conversation.

The reflections put down in this book themselves emerged from living conversations. Those conversations include, first of all, students and parishioners whose questions and insights over many years have engaged me, sometimes challenging and correcting, sometimes offering new possibilities. It is a delight when those one is commissioned to teach become teachers to the teacher! But the conversation has not been limited to students, of course. It includes colleagues in ministry who have been companions in both faith and the theological journey for a lifetime. To them all, I offer my deepest gratitude.

I reserve for special mention my own teachers and theological mentors. This is particularly the case for those who introduced me to and have accompanied me in learning the contemporary Dutch Reformed tradition. I refer explicitly to this tradition in this book, and not only because it is not well-known to many in the United States, including many who can claim that tradition as their own. I do so primarily because this tradition offers insights to the matter at hand, contributions known at most to very few in the United States. To my interlocutors in that tradition I also offer my deepest gratitude.

Finally, I express thanks to those who have assisted in the production of this book. To the editors at Wipf and Stock, as well as to the gracious people at First Church in Albany who provided space for a retired pastor to write, a thank you. And finally, to my wife, Colleen, who not only puts up with a partner who works in the solitude of a writer, but who reviewed the manuscript, correcting the inevitable and sometimes embarrassing errors.

Easter 2016

1

INTRODUCTION

It all begins in wonder. It begins in what Abraham Heschel calls "radical amazement": "wonder rather than doubt is the root of knowledge."[1] While for Heschel this is true of all knowledge, it is at the foundation of what we consider religion. It is especially when we want to talk of God that we come up against what Heschel calls the "ineffable." At that point our minds, with all our rational skill and capacity, reach a limit. "The attempt to convey what we see and cannot say is the everlasting theme of mankind's unfinished symphony, a venture in which adequacy is never achieved."[2]

Believers are overwhelmed with this sense of astonishment and of their consequent inability to articulate adequately what they witness. When the crowds witnessed Jesus, they "were amazed" (*thoubeomai*—astonished) (Mark 1:27). "The Gospel is about a series of events in which we are led from one surprise to another."[3] It is no accident that the biblical narrative is a *story* and not an argument, not a theological treatise. It is not intended as a story as we think of stories: pieces of fictional prose, spoken or written. The reports are *witness* to what has left the witnesses, if not exactly speechless, then groping for words in which "adequacy is never achieved."

The creeds and confessions of the church are repositories of astonishment, of "radical amazement." At first glance, that does not appear to be the

1. Heschel, *Man Is Not Alone*, 11.

2. Ibid., 4.

3. F. W. A. Korff, *Christologie*, 1:5, quoted in Ruler, *De vervulling van de wet*, 5. All translations from the Dutch in this book are mine.

case. They read more like dogmatic propositions that carefully delineate divine truth, as crafted as scientific discourse. The language is often highly abstract—"one essence, three persons," e.g.—and filled with technical terms like "atonement," "justification," and "sacrament." Such abstractions are learned attempts (often following very long stretches of development) to capture the mystery. But that is what they are—attempts. As such they are not without value. They are attempts because, astonished, we cannot keep silence. Captured by astonishment, we want to speak it, say it, share it. And more. As humans something within us longs to give expression that becomes praise. We long to be "orthodox"—that is, to give proper praise as a consequence of our astonishment.

CONFESSION AS WITNESS

So the proper genre of confession is *witness*. It is so in a double sense. On the one hand, it is derived, or more accurately, it is a report of what Israel and the first followers of Jesus witnessed. "That which was from the beginning, which we heard, which we have seen with our eyes, which we have looked upon and touched with our hands, concerning the world of life . . . that which we have seen and heard we proclaim also to you . . ." (1 John 1:1,3). Confessions are an attempt to summarize that witness in its essentials. It translates that first witness into new contexts of culture and language.

But on the other hand, it is also contemporary witness to the gospel. It is not only the apostles and prophets who witnessed what God is about in Israel and in Jesus. Hearing the biblical narrative, gathered in Christ's community around Word and sacrament, and energized by the Holy Spirit as believers engage in all of life, contemporary believers are also witnesses to God's work of calling them into community, offering forgiveness of sin, giving new life and new hope, and engendering a love that does not come from the human—and wondrously does. The confessions are contemporary witness.

The old creeds and confessions are indeed context-bound. Fourth-century creeds emerged in the intersection of Greek and Roman culture with the linguistic tools at hand and engaging the religious experience and needs of the church. Reformation confessions likewise reflect the religious needs and experiences of the time, which included not least of all a breathtaking shattering of the one, holy, catholic, and apostolic church. They are, in the words of the declaration ministers of the Reformed Church in America, "historic and faithful" documents.[4] That is, they are truthful expressions of the truth of the gospel within the context of their own age. But, we may ask, are they not dated? Do they not belong in the church's reliquary, there to be honored as artifacts of where the Spirit has led a particular church community through the past? Do they, can they, express current understandings or experiences of how the gospel, how Scripture, shapes and forms history today? To what extent can we *confess* them today?

As witness, Christian confessions indicate the peculiar or particular nature of the wonder that it struggles to describe. Witness is to *event* or *events*, and such take place within a history. Confessions, then, are to be distinguished from *myths*. Indeed, while Scripture has mythic elements, its narrative is fundamentally historical. A narrative myth honors the wonder by acknowledging that the eternal truth it manifests cannot be captured in concepts, but has a surplus value that escapes ratiocination. This sort of narrative, however, while truthful, does not claim to be historical. In fact, it transcends particular history. Confession witnesses to a historical reality— Israel and Jesus—and while it, like the biblical narrative, acknowledges that the wonder escapes capture, it still insists that it has witnessed something fundamentally true *in a historical gestalt*. The confession attempts to acknowledge that historical reality as extending beyond the events described in Scripture to events of the present. The substance of the confession attempts to articulate that astonishment in concepts that engage the present. As will be manifest in the confession under discussion, this is the wonder that in Jesus of Nazareth the second person of the Trinity is fully, historically present. Moreover, that the Holy Spirit, God's own self in an essential relation to this Jesus, is present and active in our history.

The genre of witness has the further implication that a confession is neither doctrinal argument nor exposition. Its statements are theological in that they are claims about God and God's relation to the world put in conceptual terms appropriate to the contemporary context and consistent with the biblical message. They do not, however, purport to make the kind of case that a fuller theological treatment would attempt. This book is a product of the latter. The confession only endeavors to describe the wonder that has happened, and more, the God who is disclosed—or more properly, the God who discloses God's self—in the events that are witnessed. A confession may, and often does, give biblical citations in support of its statements, thereby manifesting that it faithfully reflects the original biblical witness,

4. *Book of Church Order*, 128.

and furthermore tacitly indicating that the foundational authority for its claims is biblical.[5] In that limited sense, it notes the support of Scripture. Moreover, a confession also offers a particular account in its outline, its internal connections, and its dynamic flow. That is to be noted as the confession is received and reflected upon—and as later theologians and students note how these characteristics tell its own peculiar "story."

CONFESSING AS ACTION

I have asked whether we can *confess*. The formulation is carefully chosen. It does not ask about *having* a confession. Confessions are written documents, and the tendency is to treat them as documents, much like legal writings that are consulted for what they say on the page (as would a contract, for example). "Confession" is a noun that describes a written deposit. And we certainly have confessions codified in many church books. "Confess," on the other hand, is something we *do*. In confession we state or claim something. We say, in effect, "This is who we are," or "It is by this that we live." When the Confessing Church in Germany uttered its Barmen Declaration, it clearly situated itself in its world in reference to the "one Word of God" and that in contradistinction to the Germany of National Socialism (or more precisely, the German Church).[6]

Understood that way, the question whether we can confess the old documents is more urgent. It may be impossible for many, perhaps even for the contemporary church. As stated above, confessions emerge in a particular context. In his famous definition of confession, Karl Barth denoted confession in part as "a description of the provisional insight currently given to the universal Christian church . . ."[7] So perhaps we should put

---

5. This is not always tacit. The confession under consideration, the Belgic, will include a section on Scripture that claims it alone is "holy and canonical for the regulating, founding, and establishing of our faith" (art. 5).

6. The Theological Confession of Barmen can be found in *The Book of Confessions*, 309f..

7. It is appropriate to cite Barth's full definition: "A Reformed Creed is a statement, spontaneously and publicly formulated by a Christian community within a geographically limited area, which, until further action, defines its character to outsiders; and which, until further action, gives guidance for its own doctrine and life; it is a formulation of the insight currently given to the whole Christian Church by the revelation of God in Jesus Christ, witnessed to by the Holy Scriptures alone." Barth, *Theology and Church*, 112.

confessions like the Heidelberg Catechism, the Second Helvetic Confession, Augsburg, and, for our purposes, the Belgic Confession on the shelf.

But before we do so, might it be worth our while to explore just what our forbears confessed? Are they simply to be set aside? We might ask: Did the Holy Spirit not work in and through them? Are they gifts from previous generations that in their own inadequate way attempt to articulate their witness to the God who meets them through Scripture and in life? When the then Netherlands Reformed Church wrestled with the place and function of confession in the church, the new church order states that the church "... makes confession of the self-revelation of the Triune God in communion with the confession of the fathers [and mothers]."[8] The church did not confess the same words as its forbears, but "in communion" with their confession. In so doing the church honored the old confession with something more than lip service. Instead, the church acknowledges the work of the Spirit in its past, and inquires how the old confession with its witness might open vistas for the contemporary church in its own expression.

As Dutch theologian O. Noordmans puts it, the confessions move from Scripture's central testimony into the broader world. Scripture remains as it is, but the confessions move into the world—we might better say that the church moves into the world, the confessions being artifacts of what the Spirit compels the church to say—where they take part in the world's struggle. They enable the church to say what needs to be said at a particular moment.[9] As the church reflects on the older confessions, it catches sight of the traces of the Spirit's work through the church in the world. As the contemporary church listens to that interaction, it catches something of what God is about at present. Or, alternately, it finds in the old words and concepts ways to express what God is about.

THE USES OF CONFESSION

Before proceeding to inquire whether the confession under discussion, the Belgic, can either be confessed with integrity today or perhaps provides substance to a contemporary confession, it is instructive to ask just what a confession *does*. What is its use? Another Dutch theologian, A. A. van Ruler, in an essay from the 1940s, "The Place and Function of the Confession

---

8. *Kerkorde der Nederlandse Hervormde Kerk*, art. X, para. 1.

9. Noordmans, "Schrift en belijdenis," 350.

CONFESSION TODAY

As an act, confession is a *contemporary* witness by which it guides and testifies and sings. It is by its nature bound to the situation in which the church finds itself—or so Reformed churches have understood the matter, as we saw with Barth's definition cited above.[15] The church responds to God's Word as it addresses them in Scripture through the Spirit. Hence, the church will testify to the wonder anew in each age. In the twentieth century we have, for example, the Barmen Declaration from Germany, "Foundations and Perspectives" from the Netherlands, and the Belhar Confession from South Africa. These confessions are contemporary to their age, and to the extent that we still live within that age, they are so for us.

But what about older confessional writings? They were, of course, contemporary in their own time. They responded to God's Word in the context of their own age. Are they more than museum pieces, more than artifacts that we honor because they have shown us from whence we have come and have indeed shaped who we are in our understanding of ourselves as believers? Can they be confessed *today*? This extended essay is an attempt to probe that question. My answer at the outset is yes, but whether that affirmation is valid awaits not only the fuller discussion below, but the evaluation of the readers. Or more accurately, my response (or someone else's) awaits the communal affirmation of the church. Can the *church* confess in the words of the old confessional documents?

As a beginning of a response, however, I note the words from the "Declaration for Ministers"[16] that every minister of Word and Sacrament in the Reformed Church in America makes upon becoming a minister. There the minister declares before her colleagues in ministry, "I accept the Standards as historic and faithful witnesses to the Word of God."[17] The old confessions are, of course, "historic." They emerged at an earlier time, the sixteenth and early seventeenth century. More importantly for our purpose, they are identified as "faithful." That is, they give a faithful—truthful, in the meaning of the word "truth" as faithful to that of which it speaks—testimony of Scripture's story. They speak it within their context. Even though we may say it differently, and even if our hearing of Scripture's story may

15. See note 7.

16. And for candidates for ministry and for General Synod professors, for that matter.

17. This is the RCA's rough equivalent to the formulation from the Netherlands Reformed Church cited above, where the church confesses "in communion with the fathers [and mothers]."

force us to a new formulation that "contradicts" the old confession, they were not wrong. The Spirit worked with them and through them as they heard in Scripture's narrative God's Word. They articulated that Word as it addressed the issues of the day, and they responded with the conceptual tools to hand. We may—indeed we must—do so differently. (Which does not, by the way, mean that we have better conceptual tools. That would be historical arrogance. We live in a different conceptual world. Ours is not necessarily, of course, a more sophisticated conceptual world!).

Once we acknowledge that our forbears were faithful within their context, we endeavor to listen *with* them. As I suggested above, while we do not live in the sixteenth century, our world was shaped in part by that century (and all centuries). Hence, our concerns, our reading of Scripture's story, has been deeply shaped by our forbears. So we probe the confessional documents to explore ways in which they may open us to our understanding of the faith in our own day, perhaps in surprising ways. Doing so is a way of honoring our mothers and fathers. More importantly, it is to honor the work of God's Spirit as the Spirit led the church to testify to the truth that grasped them, God's truth, or "troth." The exploration of the confessions is an act of retrieval.

But it need not be simply an act of digging for a treasure that we can then extract and admire it for its beauty, not at least if we ask about confessing today. Rather, we can explore the intersection between what the confessional writings say and the context of our contemporary world. Does, for example, the understanding of the death of Jesus as "payment for guilt" have any traction in a world where guilt is understood more as a psychological problem than as a religious condition? Or is the claim that God is triune relevant to a world where horrible injustice rules, often in the name of that triune God? In this present exercise we can only wait and see. Still, we cannot cavalierly ignore the old confessions simply because they are old. Rather, we are compelled to honor them first on their own terms.

THE BELGIC CONFESSION

We concern ourselves in this study with one of the old confessions, the one commonly called the "Belgic Confession."[18] It is a sixteenth-century

18. In some places it was, and is, called the *Nederlandische*—or Dutch—Confession. It is called "Belgic" because it originated in the part of the Netherlands that was "Belgium"—and later became the country of the same name.

confession, written in 1561. It was written as a defense of the Protestant faith. Its audience was the Catholic emperor, Philip II, whose subjects were that particular band of early Protestants. As a faithful Catholic, Philip was intent on eliminating pockets of Reformation faith within his lands. This was done in the Netherlands through various agents who carried out policy on his behalf. The Protestants experienced repression, often to the point of blood.[19]

Accompanying the confession was a letter by Guido de Brès addressed to Philip.[20] In it de Brès protested that he and his fellow believers were being treated unjustly. They wanted to "demonstrate our innocence concerning the crimes with which we are charged . . ."[21] They were accused not only of bad religion, but of insurrection against the king, a charge de Brès is at pains to refute. They requested a fair hearing from the king: ". . . we humbly petition you to carefully judge this matter according to our confession of faith." As a major plank in their defense, they protested their orthodoxy: ". . . we are unjustly vilified as schismatics or as disturbers of the unity of society, as disobedient and as heretics, since we are committed to and confess not only the most fundamental points of the Christian faith that are contained in the symbols of the common faith but also the whole doctrine revealed by Jesus Christ for a life of righteousness and salvation." They are, they confessed, orthodox in faith. This is, they might have claimed, evident especially in the first articles of the confession now (supposedly) before the king.

However, they are resolutely Protestant, and they would not conceal this fact, although they claimed that this too is orthodox, at least by their light. The letter continues the appeal to orthodoxy: "This doctrine was preached by the evangelists and apostles, sealed in the blood of so many martyrs, preserved purely and wholly in the early church, until it was corrupted through the ignorance, greed, and the lust for praise of the preachers, through human discoveries and human institutions contrary to the purity of the gospel." These Protestants only want to return to the purity of the faith. They are, they claimed, constrained by Scripture to believe as they confess: ". . . we are commanded to follow God's Word alone and not whatever seems right to us; for we are forbidden to add to or to detract from the

---

19. For a full and exhaustive history of the Belgic Confession see Gootjes, *Belgic Confession*.

20. There is no evidence that it ever reached Philip.

21. References are to Kemps, "Guido de Brès' Letter."

holy commandments of the great God." So begins the "protestant" section of the confession as it opens its long discussion of salvation by grace.

Hence, the confession maintains orthodoxy (and loyalty) on the one hand while on the other hand clearly distances itself from the errors that had crept into the institution of the church. Thus, one detects both a distance taken from what we now would call Roman Catholicism, on the one hand, and from the Radical Reformation (Anabaptists and compatriots), on the other hand. The confession offers its witness in its particular historical context.

CONTEXT

The context in which the church confesses the faith today has been described as *postmodern*. That is a negative description; our world is "not modern." Modernity, a word that denotes a culture or cultures shaped by the Enlightenment project, no longer rules our thinking. But neither is our world "premodern," a return to an earlier way of thinking. I will take "postmodernity" to indicate a state of affairs in which a coherent and all-embracing narrative of the Enlightenment no longer holds sway. Roughly speaking, the Enlightenment narrative holds that humanity is becoming more and more "enlightened" by reason as the dark shadows of ignorance are slowly but surely pushed back. It is as Enlightenment thinking has lost its hold that postmodernity comes into its own. But it is more than that. There is no one "big story" that describes human history. Instead, we live countless, even competing, "little stories." There may indeed be those who cling to the story of reason's advance. They may do so. But theirs is only one story among others.

This is, of course, a problem for the Christian. We do claim to live from a "big story," the story of Israel and Jesus, an all-encompassing story that stretches from creation to the culmination of history, a story with a plot and character—primarily the God who is manifest in Jesus Christ! Moreover, a confession is itself an artifact of that great story. It will not sit well in a context that denies legitimacy to the very possibility of telling that story. Postmodernity can grant Christians the "right" to their story, but only as one story among many. That may seem to give the faith a place that appeared to have been denied it in the modern age, as reason replaced faith, or as faith was made reasonable. Still, that leaves believers discomfited. The confession will point beyond itself, and indeed beyond its context, even as it arises within its context.

So postmodern. Still, that is but an umbrella term. In fact, it simply describes a confusing landscape. There is no one way of thinking, one worldview, one religious (or antireligious) way of being in the world that shapes the context in which Christians find themselves. A number of streams run through our contemporary landscape, some of them crossing or even running against each other. I look to four different thinkers who describe our age in different ways. Some characteristics of the world they describe converge; others diverge. The contemporary human lives in a world where all the descriptions fit. It is in that world that the church offers its witness.

Charles Taylor, in his monumental book *A Secular Age*, describes the long trajectory that leads to our present situation. He uses two concepts to describe the secularity of our time. The first is that the world has become *disenchanted*. We no longer live in a universe where spirits and powers reside and effect life and history. Our world has become flat. Everything can be explained, or at least it can be in principle. We do not believe that the gods bring us weather; science teaches us the genesis of thunderstorms and hurricanes—and sunny days for the beach. But if the world has become disenchanted, the self is now what Taylor calls *buffered*. Persons have become individuals. That is, in their irreducible identity they (we) have become closed in on ourselves. The primary unit of society is not the tribe or the family or the group, but the individual. And everything must be done to protect the individual; she is "buffered." What is true and important is what is true "to me." This short summary, of course, betrays the depth and complexity of Taylor's exposition. But it is sufficient to recognize the power of its description. One need only observe the contemporary city, where rationality and individualism rule. The city is a place where buffered selves may find meaning and purpose. They may find compatriots that form communities. But these communities are fluid, and the meaning they offer persists only so long as the individual grants them their meaning.

A variation of this description is represented by Douglas John Hall, whose theological project is for a North America that is "post-Christian."[22] By that he means that it (as with the West in general) has already been Christianized. We had lived in Christendom,[23] a world where the faith influenced

---

22. This especially in his trilogy, "Christian Theology in a North American Context": *Thinking the Faith*, *Professing the Faith*, and *Confessing the Faith*.

23. The Christendom of North America is not that of Western Europe. Christendom

every area of life. We could assume, for example, that our children would be taught Christian values in public school. We built churches and waited for the people to come because everyone went to church; it was just a matter of going to the "church of their choice." This situation no longer applies. The post-Christendom world has become wealthy and comfortable. We no longer need the faith to get us through. Many are nominally Christian. They may still avail themselves of a church for a wedding or a funeral, but if it offers value, it is the value they give it.

That may ring true on one observation. But not on all. Has our world become resolutely secular? Michael Cavanaugh presents another approach. For him the "holy" remains present in contemporary culture. It has, however, "migrated." As humans, some things or some persons carry the holy. They represent something that not only transcends the mundane, but that offers "salvation" from the condition of our destitution. For Cavanaugh, the holy has migrated to the nation.[24] It is the nation—with the state—that can heal our wounds. Cavanaugh is making a larger point. It is that we are prone to *idolatry*. We need our gods (Israel with the golden calf!). And we will find gods.

It was K. H. Miskotte, already in the 1940s, who pointed to the *pagan* religiosity present in the contemporary world. National Socialism in Germany, for example, was built on the ideology of "blood and soil," a clear manifestation of pagan notions.[25] Life and the principle of life come from the earth, and from the energy that flows through the veins. "Salvation" is effected through intimate connection with those forces in nature that are nothing less than the presence of the gods. Under this reading, as with Cavanaugh, humans and their culture are irresolutely religious. There is, however, a variety of ways of being religious, from classic world religions to idolatry in whatever form.

Indeed, old religious ways of being press against the secular and post-Christian world described by Taylor and Hall. One could hardly call the evangelical and Pentecostal forms of Christianity "disenchanted." In many ways, they present what they might think of as a "premodern" view of the world.[26] Furthermore, the presence of Islam in many places in the world

---

in our continent is more "functional." It has been assumed that our culture is Christian.

24. Cavanaugh, *Migrations of the Holy*. See also Ellul, *New Demons* on this.

25. Especially *Edda en thora*.

26. That they, in fact, may well be products of modernity is another story. Fundamentalism, for example, is a child of rationalism. See Marsden, *Fundamentalism and*

offers a world that is neither disenchanted nor individualized. Christians live in a globalized world where the non-Christian believer can be found as easily next door as in a distant land.

The postmodern context, then, can be confusing and can even appear contradictory. That's what makes it postmodern! It is the world in which the Christian confesses her faith. Just what that looks like will be taken up as we ask how an old confession can witness to the present context. My purpose is not to offer an apology for the faith that meets the challenges that one aspect of the context or another presents. The question, rather, is whether the context evokes witness. That context may be different at different times. At one moment we may confess within the context of various strands of Christian faith—Roman Catholic, Baptist, Pentecostal, Lutheran and the like. At another moment we confess in a fully secularized context. The context can also shift to a world in which we are confronted by the competing claims of other religions. What does it mean to confess within the particular context where it finds itself? Does this old confession still speak, or better put, does it still express faith in Jesus Christ today?

WE CONFESS

Who confesses this faith? The immediate answer might be: the Christian, of course. Our individualistic age, with the "buffered self," has shaped us to think of belief as an individual matter. I have learned to think for myself; when I come of age, I decide what is "believable," what and who is to be trusted. And, after all, don't we confess with an "I" in the church when we begin the Apostles' Creed? "I believe in God the Father Almighty . . ." That answer is not wrong. Faith is about God's care for the person, the one who has a name, myself. The person is not absorbed into a whole. Moreover, the Reformed church's beloved Heidelberg Catechism is written in the first and second person: "What is your only comfort in life and in death? That I belong . . ."[27]

But that answer, although not wrong, is deceptive. The "I" exists as part of a "we." The person is a person only in community, in the community of the church. The Belgic begins, as does, e.g., the Nicene Creed, with a "we": "we believe with our hearts and confess with our mouths." The "we"

American Culture.

27. The Heidelberg Catechism can be found in *Our Faith: Ecumenical Creeds, Reformed Confessions and Other Resources.* The citation is from answer 1 of the catechism.

is the communion of the church. The *church* confesses. That does not mean that the person does not confess, that she cannot stand before God and in the world and fully place herself in this faith—"I believe . . ." She does so, however, only in communion with the church. This is itself a communion, a particular kind of society of persons, gathered around Christ (and so the church professes *by* Christ in the Spirit). It is the church's confession that becomes personal, even as it is persons who constitute the church. The confession is not the achievement of the lonely religious genius, nor the profession of the pious. It is a "we" that confesses.

This "we" is gathered by the Word. The church is a *creatura verbi*, to use old language, a "creature of the Word." God so speaks that God's speech gathers persons together. As we shall see in the church's confession, this Word takes concrete form in Scripture, so that as it is read and proclaimed a community takes shape around it. And, as noted above, the church responds by confessing, by doing its level best to put its testimony of what has happened, in all astonishment, into words.

This is the church catholic and apostolic. That is to say, it is the church from all places, the church around the world. As we saw above in Barth's definition, a particular confession has its roots in a particular place and time but is a "formulation of the insight given to the whole Christian Church . . ." Hence, in our case, the confession is identified as "Belgic." This confession originated in what was then the southern Netherlands. And it has its social location in the Dutch church and its offshoots (in, e.g., South Africa and the United States). But while the faith is always "local," it is not limited to the local. It is a world faith, so that when the church says "we" it says it in communion with sisters and brothers from communions of countless languages and races.

But if it is catholic, it is also apostolic: the community of faith is integral with the faith as handed on by the apostles. The "we" who confess is the church through the ages. We confess "in communion with the fathers [and mothers]." This has important implications for our confession today. First of all, we don't "make it up" on the spot. The Spirit has always been working to call believers into communion and they bequeath to us the product of their wrestling. Their context is not ours; the problems they wrestled with may be different, their language antiquated. But they did wrestle and they did come to a place of confession, and we live in their legacy. We, of course, may face different challenges, and what confronts us from Scripture is something that was not a burning issue in the past.[28] But it is equally true that the past can free us from the tyranny of the present. So that, secondly, we are opened to vistas we had forgotten, freed from imprisonment in our own ideational present. We find our self, our own personhood, within a communion much larger that we had suspected. In the present work, I will be asking how one old confession, the Belgic, may do this with us and for us.

WE BELIEVE

The Belgic Confession opens, "We believe with our hearts and confess with our mouths . . ." What is it to "believe"? According to this confession, it is not simply a matter of the brain, of the mind, of reason. It is not "holding something to be true" because it has been shown to be such to our reasoned understanding. Nor, on the other hand, is it "holding something to be true" even though it doesn't fit our reasoned understanding, as in, "I don't *know* it, but I *believe* it!" It is a "matter of the "heart." Which is not to say that it is "only emotional." Belief includes the emotional, but is not limited . In the famous words of the Heidelberg Catechism, faith is "not only a sure knowledge by which I hold as true all that God has revealed to us in Scripture; it is also a wholehearted trust, which the Holy Spirit creates in me by the gospel, not only to others but to me also, forgiveness of sins, eternal righteousness, and salvation."[29] So it is both a kind of knowing *and* a trust. For the Belgic, then, the "heart" points to the fact that this has to do with the whole self, with the core of the human creature. This is not an objective something that a person can set to the side. It engages the full person.

We said above that the confession is fundamentally witness. To say "we believe" is to witness to that which is trustworthy. In that sense, it is *truth*. Truth is that which can be relied on. Truth is that which does not slip around or run away. It stays firm. The confession will go on to identify the object of that trustworthiness. This "object" is astonishing, surprising, and more, delightful. But we discover that "it" isn't an "object." It is a subject, God, who compels us to confess this trust. Faith is itself a gift of the Spirit. The Heidelberg again: "The Holy Spirit produces [faith] in our hearts by the preaching of the holy gospel, and confirms it by the use of the holy

---

28. Consider, for example, how the Belhar Confession emphasizes themes that were either absent or underdeveloped in earlier confessions: unity, reconciliation and justice.

29. Answer 21.

sacraments."[30] We are drawn into a place where what comes to us through Scripture shows itself to us to be trustworthy. We trust those who witness, that is, Scripture itself as a chorus of witnesses. In turn the proclamation of the gospel, that story, itself wakens something within us. And we offer our own testimony in turn—the confession.[31]

But we not only "believe with our hearts," we "confess with our mouths." What has hold of us at the core of our being now finds oral articulation. We testify to the object of our faith in public. This is not a private affair, neither of the person nor of a hermitic community. The church *publicly* responds to God's address. That will require that it be put into words, into a language that communicates to its culture. It will say to the culture (as well as to God and to itself) that "this is who we are" before God and the world. Daniel Chantepie de la Saussaye Sr. noted in the nineteenth century that the confession described the origin, the way or road, and the destination of the community of Christ in faith.[32] The confession simply does so publicly.

In that way it marks out its identity. It distinguishes itself from the world around. The confession is an expression of the holiness of the church. "We" are different to the extent that we trust *this particular* God, the God who called Israel, who is manifest in Christ, and who is present in the Spirit. We have been shaped by the God who turned to God's creation and acted in love. We are *not* different in that we are full participants in sin, but we live in the astonished delight that we have been justified and are destined, with the world, for salvation. And we must testify publicly to this.

THE BELGIC CONFESSION TODAY

The following chapters offer a reading of the Belgic Confession that intends to enable the church to confess the faith by means of that confession. They ask how the "historic and faithful witness" of that confession can also be a witness in the kaleidoscope of the contexts that make up our age. In so doing, we may discover that the confession alerts the church to the gospel in ways that are underappreciated at the present. In contradistinction, we

30. Answer 65.

31. In Reformed churches, the confession of faith often follows the proclamation of the Word (the sermon). It is, then, the response of God's people, joining themselves to the old witnesses but also giving testimony to the event that has just taken place: God's encounter with God's people.

32. Chantepie de la Saussaye, "Leven en rigitng," 133, 134.

may also discover a witness in the confession that may not have been at the forefront of its sixteenth-century authors.

This is not to claim that the Belgic is comprehensive in its summary of the faith, nor even that its witness is of what is most crucial in our present age. There are themes that are missing or underdeveloped. The Belhar Confession, for example, focuses on the biblical themes of unity, reconciliation, and justice.[33] And to my knowledge, no confession picks up the biblical concern for God's creation, despite the fact that Scripture is shot through with God's care for God's beloved creation ("God so loved the world [*kosmos*]"). Nonetheless, the Belgic has functioned as a "standard of unity" for a number of Reformed churches, and has thereby shaped the theological history as well as the piety of those communions. Can the churches, and their members—confess it today with integrity?

It is my claim that it can. To support that claim, it is important to understand the substance of the confession. Hence, we shall have to take some time to understand what the confession is trying to say. Each article can be read for its own content. However, the confession is to be read as a whole, synchronically, to understand its internal context. For example, the first article, on God, cannot be read apart from the later articles that detail God's work, and thereby identify the *particular* God to whom the church is giving witness. Understanding the "historic" nature of the witness, we will ask what the confession witnesses to the current context.

The Belgic Confession is testimony to the God who turns toward God's creation in love; specifically, the God who seeks out the human creature, lost in the quagmire of her own making. This is a God who is engaged in the world's history, a God who is not aloof and distant and who does not abandon God's good creation. The confession will detail this particularly in its doctrine of salvation. It is an account of the faith that emerged in Western, or Latin, Christianity, more specifically with the concerns of the Reformation. Hence the confesses emphasizes salvation, particularly salvation by God's good favor, grace.

That said, the confession is clearly orthodox (or catholic), Protestant (or evangelical), and Reformed. It is orthodox in its opening articles as it confesses in communion with the ancient church and its creeds (the Apostles', Nicea, and Anthanasian). It is Protestant in its emphasis on *sola gratia*, salvation "by grace alone." It picks up the themes of justification and righteousness in Christ. It is Reformed as it does not "major" in justification

---

33. That confession itself does not claim to be comprehensive.

(as with the Lutherans) but speaks of both election and sanctification, as it distances itself from the Anabaptists, and offers a Reformed understanding of the church, including the church's relation to the state.[34]

---

34. On the church as "catholic, evangelical, and Reformed," see, e.g., Billings, "Rediscovering the Catholic-Reformed Tradition Today," 154–55.

2

CONFESSING A PARTICULAR GOD

ARTICLES 1, 8–11

To CONFESS THE FAITH is serious and exciting business. It is also done in astonishment, as we saw in the previous chapter. It is serious because it has to do with the fate of history. It is exciting because it opens vistas hitherto unknown. And it is astonished because that which is witnessed shatters our expectation.

In the previous chapter, I claimed that confession is in essence testimony, witness. We testify to what we have seen and heard. The confession opens with a testimony about God. By definition, it can be about no more important reality. God is our "ultimate concern" (Paul Tillich). It does so not as apologetic, not as argument, and not even as a theological reflection, but as testimony, witness to God. Moreover, it is witness to a *particular* God.

That must be made clear at the outset, because when the Belgic speaks of God in the first article, first reading gives the impression of a philosophical description of what a God must be like, if we are to talk about a God at all: "a simple spiritual being . . . eternal, incomprehensible, invisible, unchangeable, infinite, almighty . . ."[1] The adjectives appear to be the opposite of what we know natural reality to be: complex, material, temporal, etc. A God worth thinking about must be the contrary of such a way of being. Or so we might reason. We apply such attributes to the God of Scrip-

---

1. All citations of the Belgic Confession are from the translation found in *Our Faith*.

ture because that's what God must be like. And indeed, were we simply to start from the first article and follow the confession linearly from article to article, we would think from such abstractions. But testimony does not work like that.

Rather, we will read the confession as a whole, moving backward and forward through the articles. The confession does not unfold deductively, working from first principles or from a series of assumptions. Testimony does not work that way in any case. A witness stands before an event, and event that is often opaque as it happens. The reality of the event is multifaceted and can only be reported as narrative, and while narrative has its own logic, it is not linear, or it isn't if it is true to the "thick" reality in which we live.

For that reason, in this chapter I will consider articles 8–11 together with the first article. The confession testifies to the identity of the God to whom it witnesses. Who is this particular God? It is the God that the faith has identified as Father, Son, and Holy Spirit. Of itself, that sounds properly orthodox—which, as we saw in the introduction, is an important factor in this confession—but it needs further explication if we are to grasp the astonishing nature of such a claim. At the outset, though, we can note that that identification points to the particularity of this God, and will throw new light on the first article. It will also allow us to see just how we, twenty-first-century citizens of our world, share in the testimony.

THE TRINITARIAN GOD

To speak of God as Trinity is a shorthand way of talking about God as the One who turned toward this world, the One who addressed humanity, who entered and engaged history, who risked all for the sake of this world, for what we call "creation," and more, who in so doing saved, rescued it from ruin. It must be admitted that this is "shorthand," and worse. It is inadequate. It cannot capture the full reality of this God. We are in the presence of mystery, in the presence of one who escapes all description. As Augustine remarked, that which can be comprehended (literally "encircled") cannot be God.

Still, the mystery does not dissipate into the mists of silence. Something happens. This God is not silent, nor is this God hidden. This God speaks and so is manifest. So Scripture's story begins: "And God said: 'Let there be light'" (Gen 1:3). Or take the odd story related in Genesis 18 of the visitation of Abraham at the oaks of Mamre. The story begins, "Yahweh appeared to him . . ." It didn't appear that way to Abraham. Three travelers stopped and asked for hospitality. But as the meal progressed and conversation ensued, something happened. The text has it that Yahweh (!) spoke and promised a son to Abraham and his wife Sarah. This was the reiteration of the promise that had, to all appearances, been empty. In fact, a good part of the humor (and astonishment) of the story is that Abraham and Sarah were simply too old to generate children. It was simply impossible. Sarah, overhearing, knew how ridiculous the conversation had become. Yahweh responded by asking rhetorically, "Is anything impossible for Yahweh?"

The story itself is witness. It is about a God who encounters this particular human, who addresses him, speaks to him. It is drenched in mystery, but not the mystery of clouds of smoke and voices from the blue. It is an encounter with those who appear as ordinary men. There are three of them! (Without claiming this as a biblical "proof" of the Trinitarian nature of God, one cannot help but think of the Rublov icon that pictures the three, as God, dining with Abraham. It is not a stretch, however, to notice a certain plurality in the portrayal of Yahweh in this passage). This God is a stranger, an alien, the "other." That is, one who escapes all reasoning and expectation. He/they came with a purpose. It was to further the historical story. This is about promise, promise in the most down-to-earth reality—child-birth, generations. The highlight of the story, "Is anything impossible for Yahweh?," points to the jaw-dropping incursion of this God into human history.

That incursion happened—and happens—decisively in the person of Jesus Christ. So the witness to the story testifies. The article on the Trinity includes, at center, the Son who "is the Word the Wisdom and the image of the Father." This Son will be identified with Jesus Christ (art. 10). In this way, God is manifest to human knowing. But that means that it is a particular, or specific, God who is being confessed: the One manifest in this Word—the Word that is "committed to writing" in Scripture (art. 3). It is the God who spoke to Moses at the burning bush (Exod 3), who heard the cry of the slaves and acted to engage the empire, with its gods, in the liberation of the oppressed, those who had no voice, no place in all the world. It is the God who engages the powers of darkness for the sake of the lame and the blind and the poor, and the sinner (!). This is the God made manifest in the place of rejection and revulsion, as a convicted criminal in the company of criminals.

But if it is this particular God, then the church confesses that it is the Trinitarian God—Father, Son, and Spirit. The witness points to the story, to history, to events that disclose this God as the One who, in Christ and through the Spirit, turns fully to the human and to history (in fact, this God literally makes history). In so doing, the church is forced to Trinitarian language. Here it must be said that the witness is not to the Trinity as such, as though we (or those privileged among us) were somehow given a glimpse of God as "three persons in one essence." We are in the presence of mystery, but not in the sense that that we are invited into a theophany in which divine secrets are revealed. That's the case, but it isn't our primary limitation. It is simply that the story forces us to come up with a way of speaking and writing that is most adequate to the story. And, as Augustine again once remarked, we have to say something because we cannot say nothing. So the language of "persons" and "essence," admittedly non-biblical, emerges much later than Scripture's report.

The confession tacitly admits this as the article on the Trinity moves immediately to an article entitled "The Scriptural Witness on the Trinity." If Scripture is the "clearer" means by which God communicates (art. 2), then what does Scripture tell us? As it relates the story, God met the human, engaged history, as Father/Creator, as Son/Messiah, and as Spirit. In each of these encounters it is God who meets us. And then there are those moments in Scripture's narration when God meets us in more than one of these "guises" at the same time. Consider, for example, Jesus praying to the Father, or Jesus breathing out the Spirit.

One paradigmatic story emerges from the series of citations adduced in article 9: the baptism of Jesus at the Jordan. There, as Jesus emerges from the water, a voice sounds "from heaven," the voice of the Father claiming this Jesus as the Father's "beloved Son." And the Holy Spirit appears "in the form of a dove." Father, Son, and Spirit are present at one moment, in the event of the baptism of the Lord. The event is to manifest just who this Jesus is as he begins his ministry. In Jesus, we are dealing not simply with a "holy man," a prophet, a wise teacher, an embodiment of the kind of divine love that God desires of all people. Jesus may be all of that, but he is something more: in him and on him dwells the very presence and power of God. In fact, this is so in a way that the only adequate metaphor is "son." There is an "essential" relation of Jesus to the God who is Creator of all that is. In him we see who God is and what God is about; in fact, in him we see the particularity, indeed the "otherness" of this God. The story witnesses God as *triune*.

CONTEXT I

The story of Jesus' baptism occasions the addition of our voice to the witness. Article 9 opens with the difficult sentence that we garner what we know about God as Trinity "from the testimonies of Holy Scripture [which is what we expect as per article 3] as well as from the effects of the persons, especially from those we feel within ourselves." The troubling latter phrase was a later addition to the creed, and opens the possibility that experience functions as an additional source for knowledge of things divine. I wish to leave that argument to the side. But it does provide occasion to join our voice, and does so in the context of the liturgy of the church (leaving aside for the moment the question of how we might confess outside the church's liturgy).

First, the believer knows herself to be addressed. A Voice calls to her. The story becomes more than a tale once told; the story includes her. She is challenged, called, forgiven, set free, commanded, embraced. The Word is indeed Word. She is confronted by an Other who makes a claim on her. This happens in the context of liturgy as Scripture is read and proclaimed, as the law is read, as pardon is declared, as the Voice calls her into worship and blesses her as it sends her back into the rough and tumble, the sorrows and joys, of life.

Second, the believer is engaged in the sacrament of baptism. To be baptized is to be drawn into the reality of a new covenant, that something new that has broken into his world in the advent of the Messiah. It is to become a citizen of the kingdom of God. It is to be drawn into a communion, a community. That community has a very clear, humble, earthy gestalt. It is the church, a church of persons with names the believer knows and with lives that are shared. And that communion points to a deeper communion, one shaped by a Spirit who is none other than God's own self, who stamps the believer with the sign of the Messiah. Which means that the believer is engaged with this person, Jesus. Even more deeply, the person knows himself to be united with the Messiah in some way that he cannot fully grasp. In fact, he is more grasped than grasping!

Third, still keeping to the biblical narrative, the believer is welcomed at the Lord's Table. In the event of Holy Communion, the believer is liberated from the prison of the self and welcomed to the banquet. The Spirit is present, freeing—through the Word of liberation—and uniting the person into this deeper communion. The believer shares in the prayer to the Father in thanksgiving for the Son who is fully present in the Spirit. The believer experiences the intimate presence of God—as intimate as the elements enter her body—and the transcendence of God, at the same time. The believer has palpable sense of the Trinitarian reality, a reality that takes the believer into itself. She is embraced, as it were, by the fullness of God.

In this context the believer more feels the effects of the Trinitarian nature of God than he can express with words. The words used by the confession are stammering attempts to give articulation to this reality. And still they must be used. There is a great deal at stake—everything, in fact.

What is at stake in confession the triune God? We can begin with the original context of the Belgic Confession itself. As we saw, it was promulgated to make clear to King Philip II that the faith these Reforming believers confessed was the faith of the church. They were neither heretics nor sectarians. It is especially in the first articles that the confession lays out its conformity to the traditional doctrine of the church, viz., the Nicaean understanding of the faith. That issue is no less relevant today. Is the church authentic? That is, is its identity shaped by the story of the faith? It is to ask whether the "old church" with those ancient concepts is "historic and faithful." Did it faithfully render the story and the reality of God? Was it faithful to its own sources? So, to the point for the current context, is the church faithful to the God it claims that it worships and whom it claims guides and protects it?

That question, secondly, comes to the fore when encountering churches or groups that focus so much on Jesus that they are not grasped by the Father—the "God of the Old Testament"—or cannot be engaged by the Spirit. Or, alternately, churches that are so ruled by the Spirit that the Spirit loses all connection with the Messiah and his stories. Or yet again, those churches and groups that are effectively Unitarian in confessing a monist God to whom Jesus might witness, but of whom Jesus was not uniquely and fully divine. At stake is the claim that in Christ God radically turned to the world. The consequence is to understand the faith as essentially and fundamentally historical. God was in the (contingent) Christ reconciling the world. The faith is not an idea, not a worldview, not a philosophical system (although it might engage all these things).

Fourth, the confession of God as triune moves the conversation beyond the mere assertion that "God exists." The faith is about the reality of this God. It is to tilt against the idols of the world, the alternate gods who claim allegiance and obedience. This claim gains traction in the Barmen Declaration, for example. Its first article claims that "Jesus Christ as he is attested for us in Holy Scripture, is the one Word of God which we have to hear and which we have to trust and obey in life and in death." This God was confessed against a paganism that threatened the world with terror and destruction. This God was present in Christ, the "one Word of God." This is Trinitarian language.

Hence, fifth, the salvation of the world is at stake. As the German example makes clear, the acknowledgement of another god leads to destruction. Salvation does not depend on the act of confessing itself, not even in the confession (as a document). Salvation is from the One to whom it gives testimony. But without naming the name of that God—for the name indicates that it is a particular God who is being confessed—the world cannot know whom it is who provides the "way" and the "light" of truth (that on which one can rely) to the blessed future God has in mind for God's beloved creation—and its creatures.

GOD WAS IN CHRIST

Just who is this particular God? It is the God who spoke to Moses out of the burning bush, whose voice called Samuel, who sent Abram from his homeland. The confession names God as Father, Son, and Holy Spirit. This claim is sharpened in articles 10 and 11, where the confession speaks of the Son and the Spirit. This is not the only place where the confession speaks of the Son and the Spirit, of course. It does so throughout. As we noted above, we move back and forth within the confession to hear the witness in its entirety.

Indeed, the article on the deity of Christ is scarcely all that is to be said of Christ. Subsequent articles will confess the incarnation, the work of Christ, his righteousness, and so on. On the one hand, article 10 roots this faith in that of the ancient church, that of Nicaea. And if one were to work out Christology from this point, that is where we must begin. But, on the other hand, this article is placed within the context of the confession of the nature of God. To answer the question "Who is this particular God?" we point to Jesus Christ (the Messiah). And here the biblical witness offers the stunning claim that it is this person who is the "only Son of God." The God we confess has so turned to the world that in this person the "fullness of God was pleased to dwell."

But to get the full power of the claim, we need to move beyond abstraction, even the abstraction of a historical person. This doesn't simply claim that God is fully present in some person or other, but in *this* person, Jesus of Nazareth, and so fully present in what he is about and what happened with and to him. That is, this is God fully present at the cross, at the place of dereliction. This is God in weakness.[2] This is not a God whom we would invent, conceive, or even consider honorable. This is a God who is "other," but not distantly so. This God is "other" in the form of the ordinary.

THE PRESENCE OF THE SPIRIT

If this particular God turned—and turns—to the world in the person of Jesus Christ, God turns to the world in the presence of God's Spirit. Scripture's story speaks of the presence of a reality that it denotes as "spirit"—a wind or a fire—who is present where God is present. It appears in the first sentences of the Bible when the "Spirit" hovers over the abyss of the deep (Gen 1:2). The Spirit will appear over and again, inspiring prophets, anointing kings, at the conception of Jesus, promised by Jesus to his followers, and most pointedly at the first Pentecost following Jesus' resurrection, when the Spirit was "poured out" on Jesus' followers. The witness of the confession is that this Spirit is none other than the "true and eternal God." Like the Son, the Spirit is "neither made, nor created, nor begotten . . . ," of "one and the same essence, and majesty, and glory, with the Father and the Son" (art. 11).

With this testimony, the confession claims that the "sense" that followers of Jesus have of the presence and power of God is not a residual sort of influence that one might receive from a famous and worthy person—a Ghandi or a Lincoln or a Martin Luther King Jr. We can, of course, say that they, like all persons, are "spiritual" as the energy of their lives radiates beyond themselves and something of their person reaches beyond. The difference to which the confession testifies is that that something is not an emanation from Jesus—or from God. It is not that Jesus was an influential

2. Abraham van de Beek offers a graphic illustration on the cover of his book *Jezus kurios*. The cover includes the portrayal of a bit of graffiti found on the Palatine Hill in Rome. The sketch is of an ass hanging on a cross with a man nearby pointing to the cross. Beneath the graffiti is scrawled the caption, "Alexamenos worships his god."

person whose teaching remains attractive and valid. It is to claim that *God* is present now—and throughout history—in another way. God is not a figure of the past, but present, not only in our age but in the ages to come—and in whatever it is that will transcend even those ages.

We cannot, of course, consider the Spirit in the same way that we can the Messiah. The Spirit is not to be observed. The Spirit is not embodied as a human. But that is not to say that we are not in the presence of the Spirit. Consider, for example, how the Apostles' Creed puts it in its third article, the article on the Holy Spirit: "I believe . . . in the Holy Spirit, the holy catholic church, the communion of saints, the forgiveness of sins . . ." We do live in the church, in a communion that is palpable, that sustains us in the power of the gospel. We do hear the words of forgiveness, words that liberate and transform us in the midst of a guilt that cannot be shaken by any means at our disposal. We can "believe and confess" that the God we worship is the God who turns to the world still. And we confess this in the face of a world where it appears, prima facie, that "the gods are silent."[3]

THREE AT ONCE

So this God turns toward the world, and did so in the creation of the world, again in Jesus of Nazareth, and does so in the presence of the Spirit. Each time it is God's own self who is present—not a representative or a "piece" of divinity, but God, full stop. It could appear at this point that Christians confess a God who appears in different ways at different times. But that is not the case. As the story of Jesus' baptism, noted above, makes clear, the three "persons" of what we came to call the Trinity showed up at the same time! Moreover, Jesus prays to the Father, and the Father sends the Spirit to the Son. There is a mutuality occurring. And as the article on the Trinity (art. 8) makes clear, God is not divided into three. There is one God, not three. And yet the three retain distinct characteristics.

The following articles will articulate the action of the persons in creation, redemption, and sanctification. We will pay closer attention to them at the appropriate points. At this point, it is to be noted that the actions of the God who engages the created order not only acts *toward* it, as a subject vis-à-vis an object, but God acts *within* it, *already* offering the response of love and praise to God's self. We could say that this happens *within* God in the community of the Father, Son, and Spirit, and that would in fact be

3. Miskotte, *When the Gods Are Silent.*

a constituent part of the Christian confession. But the confession of God as triune says more; it claims that God is actively present in *creation's* response, most notably, but not exclusively, in the human.

This is, of course, mystery. We are at the limits of language, and all language, including the venerable language of the ancient creeds, comes up short. And yet, as we have said above, we can say nothing less. To stammer proper witness to this God, we must say this.

"DESCRIBING" GOD

If the Christian confesses the God now manifest in Jesus Christ, a God who is one and yet who acts in three "persons," what can, or even must, be said about this God? As has already been suggested, there is a limit to what we can say. We are in the presence of mystery, so that whatever we say is inadequate. Indeed, the first article of the confession is difficult because it is inadequate. But that does not mean that it is empty. The concepts gain a particular content because they point to the particular God who speaks in the Word and who proceeds in "eternal power and might" from both the Father and the Son. Each adjective in the first article is not to be interpreted philosophically. These are not adjectives that come up against the limits of what it means to be mortal, and what a God who transcends created reality "must" be like. The attributes receive their content from the story, specifically from the Word, who is the "exact image of the person of the Father." (art. 10).[4]

This God is *single*. God is the only God. This is in contradistinction to the idols.[5] This challenges and negates the pretension of other gods. These were the powerful gods who ruled the empire, Egypt, and who brought fertility and prosperity to Canaan. These are the Roman gods and their representatives, the Caesars, who brought peace to the known world. This God is not manifest in the gods that beckon our contemporaries (and ourselves), the gods of commerce or war or romance. This God is not a present version of paganism old and new.

---

4. Verboom, *Kostbaar belijden*, 51f., offers a summary of how the various attributes of God are found in later articles of the confession. For example, God's omnipotence appears in art. 26, where Christ has all power in heaven and on earth. And God's wisdom appears in art. 17, where in God's wondrous wisdom, God seeks the fallen human.

5. Koopmans, *De Nederlandse Geloofbelijdenis*, 7.

Nor is there a "God of the Old Testament" and a "God of the New Testament." That sort of claim echoes the old Marcionite heresy, to be sure. Marcionism claimed that the God of the Old Testament, the violent God, is not the same as the God of the New Testament, a God of love. Marcionism remains attractive. The Old Testament appears to relate a vengeful, punitive, and sometimes angry God, while the New Testament presents the forgiving and loving God. That caricature is, of course, completely wrong; the Old Testament God is forgiving and the New Testament God can be quite angry. But in any case, the confession claims that the Old Testament and the New witness to the same God. It may be impossible for us to remove the problem, but that is because God transcends our categories and our knowing. The encounter with this God places us in the presence of the mystery. And yet the voice of the God who speaks is clear: there is no other god to be tolerated in the presence of this God. No other god will save. In fact, all other gods are products of the human, religious imagination.

This God is *simple*. There are no "parts" to this God. You cannot analyze God by "breaking God down" into constituent pieces, looking for "something" that might constitute the essence of the divine. God is not an object and so cannot be manipulated. That also means that it is not possible to build a system into which God fits. God is not part of a system.[6] God is absolute subject. Again, this is to be understood from the manifestation of God in Christ and through the Spirit. Jesus shatters the system. The "system" tried to break Jesus, to crucify him because he defied the systems of his age. The Spirit breaks through the barriers, destroys the vessels that we construct to contain religion. The paradigmatic event of Pentecost (Acts 2) narrates how the Spirit breaks through that fundamental instrument of division, language, and so transgresses something constitutional to our humanity. The Messiah, in his body, breaks down the wall that divides Jew from Gentile (Eph 2:14), and so the institutions and cultural constructions that characterize our world. To confess God as simple in our era, then, is to eschew any talk of God that uses God for the furtherance of any of our human projects.

This God is *spiritual*. This sounds self-evident. "God is Spirit" (John 4:4). Koopmans claims that this is a way of talking about the freedom of God.[7] Here, particularly, it is important not to think too quickly that we know what this means. We think of "spiritual" as that which is invisible,

---

6. Ibid., 18
7. Ibid., 19

not bound by the material. It denotes those forces that move us inwardly, that have profound effects not only on our emotions, but at a deeper level. In the last century we learned to call that the unconscious or subconscious. But if we are talking about the God manifest in Jesus Christ and present in the Holy Spirit—that is, in God's Spirit—then the "spiritual" takes on a specific meaning. It *is* about that which transcends the material, but it is not separate from the material. This God is not caught or grasped, not even by human images or ideas. Put plainly, the God Christians worship and adore, hear and obey, is not the *idea* of God, not even the most pious idea. The God confessed is not even the God captured by the confession itself!

The *eternality* of God indicates that God is not bound by time, nor even by the division of time and timelessness. God is beyond even the concepts that surround our notion of time. Jesus, of course, was, on the one hand, bound by time. That is what it means to be human. And yet this same Jesus is *not* bound by time. Hence the first witnesses testified to both the resurrection and ascension of Jesus. This one who manifests the Son from all eternity is the Lord in all that is to come. And we know that he prayed to the Father, the one who created the very "being" of time itself. Confessing God as eternal, Christians stand before the God who was at the cross, and thereby at the place of utter dereliction—*our* places of dereliction—and *at the same time* transcends it all. Our short lives are lived in the presence of the eternal reality that is God. That would give us a sense of vertigo were it not for the fact that this God became small in order to stand beside is. In that very act, the eternality of God embraces the temporality of our days and seasons.

This God is *incomprehensible* and *invisible*. God's incomprehensibility is quite evident. Because we cannot fit God into a system, God is incomprehensible. Moreover, we cannot grasp the God whose story is told in Scripture. We cannot make God "fit." Even in the story that is before us, we're left with pieces that don't fit. We are like my younger brother who, as a young lad, would take apart our father's lawnmowers just to see how they worked. Then when he put them back together, there were pieces left over. We cannot make the God who commanded Abraham to sacrifice his son, the son of promise, "fit" with the God who in Christ welcomes the children, the lame, and the lepers. So this God is "invisible." We cannot see the full reality of this God. We can, of course, see Jesus (or could). But even then, the full reality of what he is about escapes human sight. God was fully present at the cross. The cross was an event that was witnessed with human eyes. But that it was *God* present escapes sight, until we "see" with the eyes of faith. And so witness to what cannot be seen.

That God is *unchangeable* presents a problem for the attentive reader of Scripture. Because there are reports of times when God changes the divine mind; God "repents" (e.g., Hos 11:8, 9). Indeed, there are stretches of Scripture where the prophets, for example, plead to Israel or Judah to repent so that God might change the divine plan and not destroy the nation (Jer 26). Still, Scripture's story also reports that God does *not* change (Jas 1:17). God's unchangeable nature points to the faithfulness of God, God's troth, or the truthfulness of God. You can count on God. That, indeed, is the arc of the story. The Trinitarian reality of God is all about God's loving faithfulness as the arc of God's engagement with this world is true to form, from Creator, through the Messiah and as the Spirit is manifest.

The *infinite nature* of God does not only describe how God escapes human measurement. That is indeed the case. More significantly, however, we take note of just *where* our measurement comes up short. "My thoughts are not your thoughts, neither are your ways my ways, says the Lord" (Isa 55:7). Scripture's story is of the God who continually surprises, who does not conform to human limitation, even the limitations our thoughts place on God. This is most manifest in the person of Jesus, and in the claim that as God-forsaken he is in fact the Son of God, God most manifest. This is impossible. But it is the case. This God is infinite in our very midst! Infinite within the bonds of finitude! That is not possible, but the first witnesses saw it and heard it. In the presence of this God, we stand at the edge of the abyss. Were it not for more that is to be said, this would give us a spiritual vertigo from which we could know no cure.

God is *almighty*. God's omnipotence has nothing to do with conundrums like: Can God make a rock that God cannot lift? God's almightiness is guided by love. Again, we see it manifest in Jesus' life and work, in his death and resurrection. This is God who works through the worst, who can turn even evil into good. This is the God who is greater than the gods who pretend to rule. The confession makes the difficult claim that, in the midst of a history where it looks like it will be the strongest who take the prize, God is triumphant. That where death appears to have the last word, it doesn't. That those invisible powers that drive us to self-destruction, as individuals and as societies, will not have the final say. That the kingdom of God that Jesus proclaimed *is* already present and *is* the future.

The first article takes a turn in its description of God when it moves to what is often called the "communicable attributes" of God (communicable because they are "common" to both God and humans). God is completely *wise, just,* and *good.* The *wisdom* of God is not simply that God is "all-knowing." In fact, the confession doesn't make that claim at all! Wisdom is to know how things work, and why they work that way. The wise person knows such things as the appropriate time to do something, how it is to be approached, when it is best to refrain, and the like. God's wisdom has to do with how God treats the world. The early witness testifies to how God engaged Israel, and how in Christ God deals with the lost and the last, with the sinner and the sinned against. We see God's wisdom, for example, in the forgiveness of sin, which signals that this is *God's* wisdom and not ours (forgiveness makes no sense to human reason). We see God's wisdom in sustaining a world that would otherwise have ruined itself.

And if God is wise, then God is also *just.* This is a difficult concept, if only because we have very definite ideas of the nature of justice. In fact, we have a plurality of ideas of what makes up justice. That, in fact, is a good part of the problem. We conceive what justice must be, and so we construct or establish it. But the justice of God transcends our notions of justice. Again, this justice is evident ultimately in Jesus of Nazareth. This is *God's* justice, a justice that justifies the sinner![8] This is a justice that is evident in the kingdom of God, where love triumphs and the broken are healed and the dead raised. This is justice over the long arc of history and beyond, justice within the ambience of eternity.

And finally, this God is *good,* and more, *the source of all good.* The temptation—and it has been a temptation all along—is to measure God against our notion of what counts as good. This is quite common, especially with those who reject God. There can be no God, or at least not this God, because this God doesn't measure up to what is good. We think of this God as vengeful and angry, the God who called for the destruction of the innocent. Such difficulties persist in our reflections on God—and are not strange to Scripture's story. But it is to operate out of our own notions of goodness. And the confession gives space to this move. For we do have a sense of the good. We have a conscience. But whence that notion of the good? Does it emerge from our common life—the good is what we have

---

8. See art. 23 on justification. Fleming Rutledge helpfully suggests that justice is best understood as a verb, and then meaning "to rectify," and refers to "the power of God to make right what has been wrong." *Crucifixion,* 134.

decided together is good? Or does it originate, as the confession claims, in who God is?

The confession's claim is that the one we worship and adore is good. That is, that the one who turns toward the world, the one described as Father, Son, and Spirit, is neither indifferent nor capricious, but has the well-being of the world at heart. Indeed, all the good that happens in this tired and weary world, all the good that wells up from the human heart, all the good that apparently happens by accident, all comes from this God.

Hence one can say that all that has been said before in this article about God is said in the context of the goodness of God. This God isn't only "single and simple," isn't only "eternal, incomprehensible," etc. All those descriptions are guided by the goodness of God. So that the one God to be worshipped is the God who is good. We can exist in the presence of the infinite God, we are not done in by the immensity on the edge of which we perch because this God is good. And we can confess that because this God is good.

CONTEXT II

We noted above that the context in which we twenty-first-century Christians confess is liturgical. We witness to the God who turns toward us in the context of worship. But if that were the only context, then the God we confess would be the God who meets the world in Christian worship. Given what we have claimed about this God, it should be clear that the context in which we confess is, in fact, the created order, including the full arc of human history. This is the God who engages the human *in history*, and engages that history in a particular way, with particular intentions.

This makes the confession relevant in political, social, economic, cultural, and environmental contexts. For *this* is the God with whom all these areas have to do. This just and good God, this God who is infinite mystery, is engaged. Just how this God is engaged is the subject of the following articles of the confession. At this point it is sufficient to note that the witness to the presence of this God is not silent, but is voiced by the church, of which task it is to be witness. As Karl Barth put it, God sends God's community, the church,

> . . . among the peoples as His own people, ordained for its part to confess Him before all men, to call them to Him and thus to make known to the whole world that the covenant between God and

man concluded in Him is the first and final meaning of its history, and that His future manifestation is already here and now its great, effective and living hope.[9]

9. Barth, *Church Dogmatics* IV.3.2, 681.

3

KNOWING GOD

ARTICLES 2–7

IN THE PREVIOUS CHAPTER, we noted that the church gives witness to a particular God. This God alone is God, but it is a God who does not conform to our criteria of what God must be. It is this *particular God*, the sovereign God; that is to say, it is the God who transcends human thought and imagination. As particular it is God with a name: Father, Son, and Holy Spirit. This particular God turns to the creation in act and discloses God's self to the creation. Believers witness that self-disclosure. The stretch of articles in the Belgic 2–7 have that disclosure as subject.

There is a circularity at work here. Because God discloses the divine self, we can witness that disclosure. And because we witness that disclosure, we know something of God's self. From the human side, there is a certain order: we cannot speak of God unless we have grounds for such speech, and the grounds come in how we know. So we can speak of God as one, simple spiritual being, or as triune, not because we have direct access to God, but only because we have a means of knowing. We call it revelation, for it can only be disclosed *to* us. On the other hand, we can only know because God does not remain hidden, but in fact discloses God's self. The confession begins by explicating a particular relationship between God and the creature.

THE BEAUTIFUL BOOK

The Belgic begins this section of the confession by claiming that we know God by two means. The first is through the "creation, preservation, and government of the universe," which is like a "beautiful book." God's created order leaves evidence of God's reality that is plain enough to see if we have eyes to see. Imagine that you are on a wilderness trek, far from civilization. You come upon a beautiful garden with rows of tended vegetables, flower beds scattered throughout, fountains playing in the midst. Without reflection you surmise that another human has been here before you. Moreover you know that someone is a gardener, one who cares a great deal about gardens, who nurtures and tends this plot of ground.

This simple illustration does not stretch very far. As a human stumbling on this cultivated patch of ground, I think of another human. We have a sense of what humans are like. So this doesn't work for the creation. The point is apt, though, for as we stand in the midst of the marvel of the creation, we are given to ponder: What brought this about? What or who is behind it? Is there a "who" who arranged it all in such a way? Given what was confessed in the first article, we might wonder at the goodness of it all. The created order is good!

There is, of course, a problem with that claim, a problem that will advance our reflection. But something important is afoot here, something that is all too easily missed. It was an old heresy in the church that viewed the created order, materiality, as less than good.[1] In fact, the created order is the product of a lesser God, the vengeful God of the Old Testament,[2] and salvation is the rescue of the spirit from evil materiality. But this "book" is "beautiful," the creation of the good God.

Still, there is a problem. We look around the universe and do not see God's providence and government. We see the degradation of nature, the chaos of violence, the dumb march of a bloody history. We see not only the beauty of the sunset, we suffer the horror of tsunamis and hurricanes. We not only marvel at the intricacy of the human body, we suffer from cancers and viruses and plague. So while God "authored" the beautiful book, it is hidden from our eyes and our hearts.

---

1. The Gnostic heresy maintained that material reality is evil. That Gnosticism is not a matter of the past is evident from *The American Religion*, where Harold Bloom argues approvingly that Gnosticism is the American religion.

2. The previous chapter identified Marcionism as holding to this view.

THE COMPARATIVE

The confession transcends this problem by the use of a comparative. "God communicates *more* clearly through the holy and divine Word."[3] We will identify the referent to this Word below. At this point I note that the identity of God as self-communicating is now manifest in another way. If we cannot "receive" God's self-communication in the universe present to our senses, then God has a clearer way of communicating. This will be through the Word. That is to say, in some way God "speaks," and speaks in such a way that the human can hear that speaking and, one presumes, hear it as *God's* speech.

It is a Word from God, the Word *of* God. This is said against the gods who are silent,[4] the idols of whatever age, the powers that withdraw into their mysterious silence. It is not so with this God. But more than that: this is a God who comes *to* us as other. We are not ventriloquists making God speak the words we put into God's mouth. Nor is God's communication the product of our most pious and moral thoughts. This is a Word to which we can only witness.

Because God speaks, the universe becomes transparent, and despite ourselves we can observe the universe in such a way that we do in fact "ponder the invisible things of God." The confession is not an occasion to develop a natural theology, a theology that derives knowledge of God from God's presence in the natural order.[5] For one thing, to do so would be anachronistic; it would import a category into a sixteenth-century document that was not available at the time. More importantly, the confession does not claim that there is a "connection point" in the universe (or in us, for that matter) that would allow us to think or meditate our way *to* God. The confession is about God's *self*-disclosure. Furthermore, while the reference to Romans 1 is meant to underscore the fact that the human is "without excuse" for not noticing the handiwork as God's, the book of Romans itself is clear that "all have . . . fallen short of glory" (3:23). The simple reality is that minds darkened by sin (all minds, as it turns out) cannot see God. However, because God continues to turn toward God's beloved creation—

---

3. Koopmans, *De Nederlandse Geloofbelijdenis*, 23 (my emphasis).

4. Cf. Miskotte, *When the Gods Are Silent*.

5. This, of course, was occasion for a loud and influential debate within Reformed theology, to which the names Emil Brunner and Karl Barth are attached. To Brunner's assertion that there is a "connection point" in creation between God and the human, Barth issued his curt *Nein!* For Barth and his followers, natural theology is not possible.

as the confession will go on to outline in detail—our eyes are opened to "read" God's "beautiful book."

How so? Through the Word. Since this stretch of the confession will go on to talk about Scripture, it is important at this point to identify the Word as something distinct, but not separate, from what we have come to call "Scripture." We have already met that identification in thinking of the nature of God. In Article 8, on the Trinity, the Word is identified with the second person of the Trinity, the Son. Hence, the primary referent of the Word is God's Word is the Son, the one who becomes incarnate in Jesus Christ.[6]

God communicates through a person born into our history. What God has to say can be read off the presence, the action, the words of this human. This will say a great deal, and we shall have to explore that as the confession unfolds. At this point, however, two things can be said. The first is that what God has to say is "as much as we need in this life for God's glory and for our salvation." That is a great deal, but it is not everything. God does not disclose all that is true, nor does God communicate all the secrets of the universe. On the one hand, there is a good deal that is mysterious and beyond our knowing. That is by definition true of God's own self. On the other hand, there is a good deal that is true that we discover on our own through science and art, even much that enhances life and gives joy.

Still, that is a lot. God's glory and our salvation include the fact that we are "saved" in order that we might delight in God's glorious creation. In the person of Christ we can see, for example, that God intends good for the creation. The curtain of our own self-interest is drawn back and we can see the wonder for what it is, and can indeed reflect on the One who is behind it all. Knowing that this God holds nothing back in Christ, we can see just who this God is, and so enjoy the creation as the work of the One who is "good and the source of all good." If we take the step that will be taken in the following article of the confession and note that the Word is also "written down," that is, in Scripture, then with John Calvin we can stand in awe as we read the book of creation through the lens of Scripture.[7]

---

6. Note that I stated that the *primary* referent is the second person of the Trinity. There are places in the Belgic where "Word" refers to Scripture as the "revealed Word" in "writing" (e.g., art. 13, 24, 29, 36, and 37).

7. Cited in Koopmans, *De Nederlandse Geloofbelijdenis*, 26.

THE CANON

While the Word is Christ, it refers not *only* to the figure of Jesus of Nazareth. In fact, the confession continues, God "spoke" through men and women moved by the Holy Spirit (citing 2 Pet 1:21). God communicates God's self through *human* speech. God "accommodates" the human, to cite Calvin.[8] What we call "Scripture" is the record of that speech, a record that can only be preserved in written form. Hence, so the confession continues, God "commanded" that revealed Word to be written down. We have God's Word in writing.

Hence a fundamental claim of the Reformation: *sola scriptura*, "Scripture alone." The Bible is the Word of God, and the Bible *alone* is to be the measure against which all doctrine, and indeed all life before God, is to be measured. In fact, in the polemics of the era (and very much into our own age) the Bible was set against other "sources" of knowledge of God, primarily Tradition (with a capital T), but also reason and experience, to name two other alternate sources. But just what does this confession claim about the Bible? While it confesses that God is the author of the "good book," how can it make that claim, other than simply baldly asserting it?

As the Reformation took hold, particularly in the seventeenth century, a number of doctrines concerning the Bible itself began to develop. Various theories of inspiration were proposed.[9] That, however, came later. In fact, the Belgic itself and as such does not have a doctrine of Scripture. It can be argued that it presents a torso or a beginning of what might grow into a theory concerning Scripture. Moreover, it has a good bit to say about Scripture. But it does not present a criterion by which one can say "this is Scripture" and "this is not." As A. A. van Ruler put it in claiming the Scripture as the Word of God, the church says something substantial, not formal. That is, the claim is not that it is a book of a certain *kind*, and therefore that it communicates God's Word, but rather that in hearing the content of Scripture, what Scripture says, the church hears God speaking.[10]

This becomes clear from within the confession itself when we examine how it deals with the *canon* of Scripture. Article 4 identifies those books that belong to the canon of the Old and New Testament. By contrast, article 6 identifies books that belong to what is commonly called the Apocrypha,

---

8. Calvin, *Institutes*, IV.3.5, 8.

9. Heppe, *Reformed Dogmatics*, 17.

10. Van Ruler, "Vormen van omgang met de bijbel," 337

books that do not belong in the canon. At first glance this is puzzling. We are in the sixteenth century. While the development of the canon in the earlier centuries of itself may be of interest, was it not the case that Christians had a Bible in hand by the sixteenth century? It is, of course, true that the church's Bible included the apocryphal books and that the Reformers found it necessary to distinguish a "true" canon such that those books would be excluded. But why? And how does that help us understand how God communicates through Scripture?

The article on the apocryphal books offers a clue. The confession allows such books can be edifying so long as they agree with the canonical books. But it goes on that "they do not have such power and virtue that one could confirm from their *testimony* any point of faith or of the Christian religion" (emphasis added). They do not *witness* to the narrative that bears within itself a power to save. They are not themselves God's speech to God's people. It is the *content* that convinces.

This is the authority that adheres to the teller of the story, to the author of the narrative. Here we might naturally think of God as the author. But the human writers of Scripture are the narrators. They possess the authority of the eyewitness, of the teller of the tale. And it is a tale that must be *told* because it cannot be known in any other way. As Van Ruler again puts it, there is something "non-sensical" about the tale. It is that a "savior has come as an historical reality and thus salvation is present, on the one hand for the individual Christian in her lost existence and that with a view to eternity, and on the other hand for the communion of persons and for all created reality and that with a view to the eschaton."[11] When the church hears those books that are identified as canonical, it hears that strange and wondrous story.

The process of canonization is the work of the church. In that sense the claim made by Roman Catholics that the church exists prior to Scripture as we have it is correct. This confession itself is witness to that reality. On the other hand, the logic of the confession is that the Roman claim, while *historically* correct, is not *theologically* correct. For it is the narrative *itself* that moves the church to recognize a particular set of books as canon. The authority of Scripture is not decided by the church beforehand. Nor, we might add, does it come from a claim we make about Scripture rooted in a particular view of inspiration.

---

11. Van Ruler, "Schriftgezag en kerk," 316.

In this context, Verboom notes that srticle 5 begins with the words, "we receive these books . . ."[12] These books come to us and we hear God speak through them. We do not construct or choose what will count as Scripture. It comes *to* us and we only receive it. Verboom reflects on the surprise and wonder De Brès and his compatriots sensed as they opened Scripture afresh in the context of a religious world dominated by the authority of a centralized church.

THE AUTHORITY OF SCRIPTURE

Indeed, the confession goes on, in Article 5, to state that we believe "without a doubt all things contained in them [N.B., not "about" them]—not much because the church receives and approves them as such but above all because the Holy Spirit testifies in our hearts that they are from God, and also because they prove themselves to be from God." It is not on the basis of the authority of the church that we believe the content. This is, of course, a theological claim. As a matter of fact, many first hear the story as the church tells it and believe it because, as children, say, they trust the words of the church. That, however, is not the theological basis for Scripture's authority. The confession begins by noting the "internal testimony of the Holy Spirit," the *testimonium spiritum internum*.

This sounds like a radical individualization of how Scripture speaks. This is especially so given the common notion that the Reformation was about taking the Bible from the church and giving it to the individual believer. There is an element of truth to that common understanding, but it foreshortens what is being claimed here. Note, first, what is being said within the larger context of the confession. The confession witnesses to the God who turns toward God's creation, and that to the human. God does not remain silent but discloses God's self. This happens now, not only through the Word, the second person of the Trinity, but through the Holy Spirit, "the eternal power and might proceeding from the Father and the Son" (art. 8). God comes to the human, then, in two ways simultaneously: the words of Scripture and the presence of God's own self as those words are read and heard.[13]

---

12. Verboom, *Kostbaar belijden*, 95.

13. It is interesting to note a parallel with the Heidelberg Catechism's Q/A 65. To the question, "It is through faith alone that we share in Christ and all his benefits: where then does that faith come from?" the catechism answers, "The Holy Spirit produces it

It is also to be noted that we tend to read the confession, and this portion in particular, through the lenses of our very individualized view of the world (one admittedly furthered by the Reformation itself!), so that we consider reading a private affair. I sit by myself with a book and read it. On that view, the "internal testimony" would be limited to how the Spirit works with each individual. That reading cannot be denied. However, that is not the only way, and indeed perhaps not the primary way in which Scripture is read in the church. A *public* reading takes place in the liturgical gatherings of the church. It is also a public reading in the many Bible circles and study groups that gather around Scripture. In that case, the testimony that is "internal" emerges from the communion of listeners. It is the Spirit present among the hearers who now discern the voice of God. One is reminded of the story of the first Pentecost, when on the outpouring of the Holy Spirit the first apostles began to speak in other languages "as the Spirit gave them ability," and the crowd gathered in the city for the feast was "bewildered, because each one heard them speaking in the native tongue of each" (Acts 2:4, 6). The story becomes public and it is heard by virtue of the Spirit, who makes it so public that it transcends the natural barrier of language (and hence culture).

The authority of Scripture, then, comes from Scripture as it speaks, or as Christians hear God speaking through it. It is "self-authenticating," or as theologians say, it is *autopistis*. The Synoptic Gospels report that when the people heard Jesus they were "amazed" because he "spoke as one with authority" (Mark 1:22). It was in the speech itself. The authorization could not be proven by means of argument. Hearers could testify not only to what they heard, but to the truth of what they heard.

But that is not only the witness of Jesus' first auditors. It is our contemporary witness as well. We cannot prove that Scripture's narrative comes directly from the mouth of God. We can, however, acknowledge that in it we hear a strange story, a tale that we would never, and could never, devise. And yet we hear in it a power that has saved us from despair, that has offered hope in the midst of darkness, and that has beckoned us to live in ways that look to violate all self-interest. These are words that have freed us from prisons of our own making, that open us to the wonder of reality, and that allow us to be ourselves, human. We can only testify to times and moments when those words have called us back from the brink, have

---

in our hearts by the preaching of the holy gospel, and confirms it by the use of the holy sacraments."

challenged and shattered our easy self-confidence and brought us to the deeper reality of what God is about in the world and all creation.

A "making known" takes place in the reading of Scripture. The theological term is "revelation." Something not seen or known is disclosed, made known. It cannot be forced, but "shows itself." At the same time, we experience a sort of recognition: "Of course, that's the way it is." We couldn't have said this prior to the disclosure, but once seen, life becomes transparent in a way that it hadn't previously. The confession is getting at something like this when it says that "even the blind are able to see the things predicted in them do happen." This prediction need not be considered bluntly, as the biblical forecasts that have come about, rather like Old Testament "prophesies" have been pegged to the arrival of Jesus of Nazareth. The trajectory runs more deeply. It is that when we read and hear Scripture, our world—and ourselves—become transparent. We see clearly, for example, that the "wages of sin is death" (Rom 6:23), or that sowing violence means "reaping the whirlwind" (Hos 8:7). We live Jesus' promise that his "burden is light," (Matt 11:3), that we may "fear not." Scriptural narratives do not remain in a past, but are startlingly contemporary. This is the self-authenticating nature of Scripture that convinces us despite our dullness.

TRUE GUIDE AND NORM

It is itself to be remarked that in this "second book," what we know about God is mediated by humans. To speak in terms used by contemporary theology, to think of God above we can only begin from below. However, that cannot mean that we talk of God from what our best minds or most pious thoughts think God to be, or *must* be. We would then be vulnerable to the nineteenth-century theologian Feuerbach's accusation that we project onto God our own notions of human perfection. The confession maintains that the "below" here are words of human authors. Moreover, these words become a guide we can trust and the norm for what we say and think about God.

The confession contrasts the Bible to other documents, customs, common sense, or shared opinion. The problem is that "all human beings are liars by nature and more vain than vanity itself" (art. 7). This does not mean, of course, that every human constantly manufactures untruths, intent on deception. No, the reality is that since all of us are sinners (art. 15), we are "vain." That is, our thoughts, even our best thoughts, reflect self-interest.

The result is that even the most edifying literature is not, finally, to be trusted. That is not to say that it has no value, or even that it is wrong. It is to say that it can be trusted only against a certain measure, and that measure, finally, is Scripture. Hence, *sola scriptura*.

A word about *tradition* is in order here. This has to do, on the one hand, with the original context of the confession itself, and on the other hand, with a common misunderstanding, particularly among Reformed Protestants, of the place and use of tradition. Early Protestants intended to "reform" the church by sorting through ecclesiastical practice that claimed for its authority the "tradition" of the church. Church leaders could, and did, appeal to Scripture, but also appealed to a continuing tradition of the church. Hence believers were part of a vast institution that included a variety of practices that claimed divine authority. The problem was that believers could be required to engage in a number of practices that impinged directly on their eternal salvation. The Reformers were about a radical housecleaning, and did so by claiming that only that which is in Scripture is "as much as we need in this life for God's glory and our salvation" (art. 2). Consequently, the confession rejects any source for knowledge of matters salvific other than Scripture.

On the other hand, Reformed Protestants did not, and do not, reject tradition altogether. A good deal of church practice is rooted in tradition. A short list would include such matters as Sunday observance, the sacraments, liturgical practices, and even the confessions themselves. To make matters more complex, there are traditions of scriptural interpretation that have held sway. To take only one example, Reformed Christians tend to read the Gospels through Pauline lenses.[14] I am not claiming that such a reading is incorrect; my point is that it is itself rooted in a tradition.

This latter point is not to negate the confession's claim of scriptural authority. As venerable as a tradition may be (even Sunday!), it always stands under the critique of Scripture. Reformed Christians who confessed the faith in the words of the Belgic Confession (or any other) were clear that should scriptural objection be brought to bear on the confession, and shown to be valid, the confession should be changed. Furthermore, despite considerable ecumenical progress in discussions of the relation of Scripture and tradition, the Roman Catholic Church retains an understanding of authority that surpasses Scripture. The pope has the authority to declare doctrinal

---

14. This practice itself has a deep history. The Latin, or Western, church has interpreted the gospel soteriologically. This in contrast to the Eastern church.

truth. Despite the fact that this authority has rarely been invoked—only twice since Vatican I, both times on Marian doctrine—it remains in place.

CONTEXT

I noted above the context in which this stretch of the confession emerged: the Reformation claim of scriptural authority against any and all competing voices. The contemporary context presents challenges that, at first glance at least, appear to be quite different. The issue for contemporary culture is not between Scripture and church tradition. The issue is authority itself. What authority can compel us?

For a very long time, the Enlightenment project located authority in rationality. This is not simply reason as such, but includes the notion of empirical verification, on which the project of modern science is built. We granted authority to that which could be verified by human rationality. This project has come under fierce criticism in the last decades. It is not my purpose to detail this long story (a task done finely and in detail by many others[15]), nor to evaluate either the Enlightenment or its critics.[16] The question is: After reason, what? Does authority rest with the most powerful?[17] Is it a matter of economics: the truth is what sells on the market? Or are we left with ourselves along with, perhaps, our tribe? Is there an authority that rests in something other than ourselves? Is there a truth that *liberates*, that frees us from a chaos of competing claims? To ask such questions is, perhaps, to set the stage for a flight to authority, a flight from freedom, to find a place where all is settled. That is the danger of tyranny, and sacred texts can themselves function as tyrants.

"Authority" suggests an "author." Who wrote the story? Which is to ask, who knows the story? Christians claim that in Scripture they hear the story from its author. That claim, of course, can be heard as a reflection of the story that Christians want to hear, a sort of projection of their own longings, perceptions, needs, inclinations, etc. Indeed, it has too often been the case that we Christians have read ourselves and our own prejudices into the scriptural story, with terrible and hurtful consequences. Consider

15. See, e.g., Charles Taylor's *A Secular Age*.

16. Although I think the critics go a bit far. I, for one, am glad for such things as antibiotics and indoor plumbing.

17. A question that Plato raised already in the *Gorgias* in Socrates' long dialogue with Callicles.

slavery, for example. However, Scripture's story is not so easily tamed. At its heart is the story of the human rejection of God. It is a story that *judges* as well as *liberates,* even as its judgment is itself liberation. It is a story that challenges our desires and self-image. We hear in the story an alien tale, one that runs against the grain of political and cultural arrangements as well as our own religious self-understanding. In hearing the story that way, we hear a Voice not our own. And that Voice beckons us into a story that is good news indeed, that gladdens the heart, that encourages weak souls, that propels us into places where we would not otherwise go, and that frees us to love.

Let me illustrate from my own recent experience of church attendance. Having been a parish minister for forty years, I have had few opportunities to sit in a pew and listen—I was always the one speaking! Of late, I have been privileged to experience worship as one of the congregation gathered to listen and to pray. I have little desire to become a sermon critic (knowing all too well the difficulty of the task). I have, however, noticed that I become impatient when someone is put in the pulpit to talk about something other than Scripture's offering for the day. While it is fine to hear the report of an inspiring project or the testimony of someone's "spiritual journey," I need something else. It clearly is not to have my own opinions or religious feelings validated. Like everyone else, I appreciate agreement with my own considered opinions. That is not, however, what I need. I long for a "strange" word, a new word, a word that will liberate me—and my culture—from captivity to the regnant gods. What will free us from the frantic rush to a success that will justify our existence? What will liberate us from the anger and violence that have captured our Western world? Who can offer a word of forgiveness that frees me from what I have done, or left undone, the consequences of which I cannot undo?

The confessional claim, the testimony, is that through Scripture that liberating word in fact has been spoken, and it has been spoken in Scripture's story.

4

GOD'S GOOD CREATION

ARTICLES 12–15

WITH ARTICLE 12, THE confession turns to the action of God with the world. The church confesses that God engages the created order; God gets involved in history. The confession of the nature of God as Trinity already signaled that fact. The remaining articles articulate the nature of God's engagement with creation.

As I noted at the outset, the confession is to be read dialectically. The articles under discussion in this chapter focus on creation, including the creation of the human. It is easy to consider this the work of the first person of the Trinity, the Father. Indeed, article 12 says just that ". . . the Father, deeming it good, created . . ." But these articles are to be read in the full context of the confession and so include the work of the Son and the Spirit.[1] Only so can we gain a full understanding of what is being confessed in the articles under consideration. This will become clear as we consider the articles in greater detail.

CREATION AS AN ARTICLE OF FAITH

It might seem odd to *confess* God as creator. After all, Paul's well-known words from Romans assert that "ever since the creation of the world [God's]

---

1. The old church would put it in a Latin phrase: *opera trinitatis ad extra indivisa sunt*—the works of the Trinitarian God, directed outward, are one.

invisible nature, namely his eternal power and deity, has been clearly perceived in the things that have been made" (Rom 1:18). Even unbelievers can know that the universe is *created*, hence a Creator exists. This would certainly be the case with adherents to many non-Christian religions. However, the confession states that it is the *Father* who created. It is not a "demiurge," a creator-god, but *this* God, the one who was confessed in the earlier articles, the God revealed in Scripture's story.

For that reason, some things are confessed about the created order. The first thing is that this is the first thing that is said about God's action with the world. That might appear obvious. Creation is chronologically first. Before the creation, there was nothing, not even time by which to measure a "before." But something more is said here. The context of the confession is, of course, the Reformation in Western Christianity. In that context, the emphasis of the confession will fall on salvation, and on salvation as God's atoning and justifying action at Golgotha. That would appear to be the primary thing: salvation in Christ. But what is being saved? It is the human, the human who was created good and the human who stands within the good creation. By confessing creation first, a claim is made about being, existence. Existence is prior to salvation, and is so in the biblical canon. And so, in an important way, being is more basic than salvation. It is the human *being* that is saved—to be what it is meant to be—which will be made clear as the confession progresses.[2]

Second, by using the term "creation," we have made a theological claim. It is that reality is not neutral. It is not "nature" that simply exists in brute factuality. All reality around (including reality that escapes our senses) comes into existence from God. More than that, because it is created by *this* God, the God who is "good and the source of all goodness," the created order is good. The Father "deemed it good" to create both heaven (reality that escapes our senses) and earth. Creation is good, but its goodness is not inherent. It is good because God deemed it good. One only need note the repeated "God saw that it was good" in the liturgical narrative of creation in the first chapter of Genesis. To confess that reality is good cuts off all notions that what is bad is rooted in materiality. To put it another way, it cannot be maintained that the material is lesser, or even that the body is a lower order of "nature." Nor is the material the locus of the powers of evil. The material can, of course, tempt the human to consider all reality as

---

2. Of course creation itself is to be redeemed (see Rom 8:19–22). But the Belgic focuses on the salvation of the human.

material, or regard the self as only body. But that is another matter, for it is also the case that we can be tempted to understand reality as fundamentally spiritual, or non-bodily.

Third, created reality is not divine; God does reveal God's self in and through creation. The creation can be the bearer of God, as is the case in the incarnation and the outpouring of the Holy Spirit. But the creation is not itself divine. As noted above, God has attributed goodness to it. But nothing in creation is to be worshipped, nor is creation itself an object of worship. It was called into existence from nothing. It does not abide on its own. It is the product of the free act of the One who turned toward the world.

Fourth, this is creation "by the Word—that is to say, by the Son." The dialectical reading of the confession is explicit here. We are claiming something about creation by citing the Gospel of John's well-known prologue that "all things are made that were made through him [the Word]" (1:3). What God is about in creation is fundamentally rooted in the second person of the Trinity. But that person was made flesh in Jesus Christ, and his incarnation is the full revelation of God. Hence, we can see something of God's purpose in creation as we look to Christ and through Christ we are given the Spirit through whom we can perceive where God is "going." The Gospels, particularly the Synoptics, tell us that the Messiah is about the "kingdom of God" that is "at hand" (e.g., Mark 1:15). The picture of the kingdom portrayed in the Gospels thus discloses what God is about already in creation.

If everything that is not God is created, we are tempted to see the world as it is as good. Indeed, there is something world-affirming in the confession of creation. Still, not is all as God intends it to be. God has intentions for creation, intentions that have been thwarted by the free creature, the human. We can catch a glimpse of the original "blueprint" in the person and work of Jesus Christ. Still, this same Jesus must go the way of the cross. The kingdom manifest in his presence meets deadly opposition. By confessing that the Father created by the Word, the church affirms the created order as rooted in the goodness of God and at the same time looks forward to the fulfillment of God's intentions *for creation*. In this way, the confession is not limited to the salvation of persons as God's sole intention. God turns toward *creation*, a reality in which the human is given a particular place, but is not the sole object of God's love.

CREATION AS RELATION

By confessing that the Father created "by the Word," the Belgic makes a further theological claim about creation. God spoke the creation into existence: "And God said, 'Let there be light'" (Gen 1:3). God *called* creation into existence. Creation is a divine "speech-act." "By the word of the Lord the heavens were made . . ." (Ps 33:6). This signifies that while creation is not divine, it exists in relation to God. It is *willed* by God and stands in a particular relation to God.

As the Belgic puts it, creatures are given particular being, form, and function to "serve their Creator." In fact, they are sustained and governed by God that they might serve humanity and "that humanity may serve God." The confession does not detail what that service consists of, but it does open up to a mutuality of relationships within creation, among humans (themselves created), and of all creation to God. As called into existence, created reality is desired by God, and so lives in gratitude to God. At the same time, the creature does not live separate from God, but in service to this same God who is "good" and who out of God's "goodness" created the heavens and the earth.

THE POWERS AS CREATED

If all that is not God is created, then nothing created can claim to be absolute. The confession expresses this in words that sound quaint to an Enlightenment and post-Enlightenment sensibility. The Belgic talks about angels that are created "good," and also about those that have fallen, "devils and evil spirits are so corrupt that they are enemies of God and of everything good." Angels and devils were part and parcel of a sixteenth-century social imaginary. They have fallen away for many in a secularized world. But that doesn't mean that the confession is antiquated.

A number of twentieth-century studies have investigated what Paul might have meant when he talked about "principalities and powers," *arche*, etc. Acknowledging that Paul's cosmos included the existence of powers that we cannot accept, scholars have probed to way of understanding that our world includes realities that transcend the material. Hendrikus Berkhof said it this way:

> In the light of God's action Paul perceived that mankind is not composed of loose individuals, but that structures, orders, forms

of existence, of whatever they be called, are given us as a part of creaturely life and that these are involved, as must as men themselves, in the history of creation, fall, preservation, reconciliation, and consummation.[3]

More recently, New Testament scholar Walter Wink spoke of the "interiority" of the realities of our existence. When talking about Satan, for example, he claims that this figure is

> the archetypal representation of the collective weight of human fallenness, which constrains us toward evil without our even being aware of it. It is a field of negative forces which envelops us long before we learn to think or even speak, and fills us with racial, sexual, and role stereotypes as if they were indubitable reality itself." "Satan is the real interiority of a society that idolatrously pursues its own enhancement as the highest good.[4]

The powers need not be evil or bad. The confession speaks of "angels." Hence, we can consider such things as the idea of freedom, or the force of equal rights. Alternately, the forces that exist could function for good or evil. Consider how some talk about the reality of the market or even of the state. Or, more politically, one can think of patriotism or nationalism. The point of the confession is that none of these realities can be considered absolute. None of them can stand over and against God. As a matter of confession, they exist within God's providential power and can, and will, be turned toward God's good ends.

PROVIDENCE

It is paradoxical that belief in a providential God has been seen as both a minimal, and hence unproblematic, way of understanding the transcendent reality of divine reality and, at the same time, as deeply problematic. Perhaps the paradox is not as sharp as it first appears. If one holds to a general notion that a divine "hand" guides reality, that a God exists who guides the fortunes of persons and history, then even if it is difficult to accept the divine presence of God in Christ—that is, accept the Christian (and Jewish) God—one can still remain "religious." The problem emerges when events are not transparent to the guidance of a benevolent divinity. In the face of

3. Berkhof, *Christ and the Powers*, 66.
4. Wink, *Unmasking the Powers*, 24, 25. Cf. Gunton, *Actuality of the Atonement*, 166.

horrific tragedy, of natural disaster, or of inexplicable human cruelty, one is faced with what has been called the "problem of evil": the existence of evil in the face of a putatively good and all-powerful God.

It is significant that the Bible knows this problem deeply. A number of psalms give voice to the complaint that God appears to be indifferent to the plight of God's children and allows the "wicked to prosper." "But as for me, my feet had almost stumbled, my steps had will nigh slipped. For I was envious of the arrogant, when I saw the prosperity of the wicked" (Ps 73:2–3). It may be very difficult for believers to confess faith in the providential action of God. In fact, because they have confessed the *goodness* of this God who "sustains and governs" all creatures, it may be more difficult.

It follows from the fact that God created the universe and all its creatures, and that *this* God turns to the world, that God did not abandon the creation to "chance or fortune." History does not proceed either willy-nilly nor by the fortunes of human endeavor. In fact, history exists; events move *toward* an end. We are not caught in a repeating cycle of events. But if that is the case, then what is to be said concerning the horrors that befall humanity, either in one's personal life (the death of one's child, say) or in natural disaster (a tsunami that kills thousands) or in human depravity (think only of the Holocaust)?

A. A. van Ruler met this difficulty full on when he claimed that "God is hidden in his providence."[5] God does not appear provident in the tumult and terror of this world. We can only know God as provident through the biblical narrative. In fact, Christ is necessary. "The foundation of God's providence lies in the salvation of the world and in life through the completed work of Christ."[6] We can only *believe* in providence; it is a matter of confession. God acts in ways that "surpass human understanding." In fact, the providential nature of God's care emerges from God's future, that future to which God is going. As we noted above, we are given glimpses of that future in Christ. We confess that God is not finished with this world. As the confession has it in our article on God's providence, God did not create the world and leave it to itself. God continues to engage it.

Because this confession has already witnessed to God as triune, as Father, Son, and Spirit, we can trust the future. That is, we can go beyond what God has done in Christ to what God is doing and will do in and through the Spirit. If God's engagement with history did not end with creation, neither

5. Van Ruler, "Gods voorzienigheid," 130.
6. Ibid., 131.

did it end with the Messiah's presence on earth. It does indeed continue in the Messiah's session with the Father, but does so as well in the work of the Spirit.

Confessors can testify to a double witness. On the one hand, we can (or some of us can) testify to the fact that God has sustained us through extremely difficult times. Moreover, we have witnessed how the dark times in history have been overcome. We make that claim even as it offers no excuse to those who perpetrated evil—or to ourselves as we have permitted it, perhaps by our silence. Our confession is of a *faith* that God rules the course of history as it moves to the future.

On the other hand, we can testify to the comfort that we have known. We have been sustained by the power of God's Spirit in the knowledge that even the worst will not overcome us. And even as it does—and we are, after all, human—we are not abandoned by the God who knows us intimately (God numbers the hairs on our head [Matt 10:30]).

CONTEXT

The sixteenth-century context of the Belgic articulates the common Christian perspective of God as creator and sustainer of the world. In its address to Philip II, it claims that its adherents are orthodox in faith. The good God created the world from nothing by means of God's Word. The confession will move from this common belief to more polemical matters—about salvation—in articles yet to come. The confession is not primarily concerned with the created order as such.

That said, the early twenty-first-century context is quite different, and differs in a number of relevant ways. First, we live in a post-Enlightenment age. It is, in Charles Taylor's words, "a secular age." Ours is the age of science and technology. We think instrumentally, and "nature" has become material to be manipulated to desired ends. In Taylor's reckoning, the world about us has become "disenchanted." Moreover, we have become "buffered" as individuals. That is, we live radically individualized lives in a world that is no more than material for whatever will benefit our buffered lives.

Secondly, and not unrelated to our first observation, we face environmental degradation. Perhaps the greatest challenge of the age is what has been called "climate change."[7] What Christians call the created reality is under threat. Is this simply a matter of survival, for humans or for the

7. See Northcot, *A Political Theology of Climate Change* , among many others.

planet? Or is it a theological issue as well: Does God allow God's own good creation to be destroyed? Can Christians continue to confess that we know an "unspeakable comfort" because God watches not only "over us with protective care" but "all creatures" as well? Do humans bear responsibility for this? And if so, how so?

It is to be noted that no church confession addresses this crisis directly. There has been no claim that we are in a *status confessionis* in this matter.[8] This despite the fact that Scripture itself is rife with the theme of the centrality of the created order to God. To cite only two instances, one from the Old Testament and one from the New, consider a prophet and an apostle. Hosea concludes his excoriation of Israel for their practice of injustice—"There is not faithfulness or kindness, and no knowledge of God in the land; there is swearing, lying, killing, stealing, and committing adultery; they break all bounds and murder follows murder"—by pointing out the consequences for the created order: "*Therefore* the land mourns, and all who dwell in it languish, and also the beasts of the field, and the birds of the air; and even the fish of the sea are taken away" (Hos 4:1–3, emphasis added). In the New Testament, the apostle Paul, in reflection on the work of the Holy Spirit with believers, notes that "the creation waits with eager longing for the revealing of the children of God . . ." for "the whole creation has been groaning together in travail until now . . ." (Rom 8:19, 22). The creation awaits liberation! Biblical themes that have long lain dormant speak freshly to our age.

Despite the fact that the articles on creation and providence were commonplace in the sixteenth century, they can be confessed with a new vigor in our age. To confess the environment as God's good creation is to claim that what happens in and with creation matters to *God*. Hence the created order is not material to be used or manipulated at will. The creation is God's delight, and hence it is to be enjoyed for its own sake.

To be sure, the created order is not divine. This is to be said against all versions of paganism that would elevate creation to divine status. Nonetheless, the creation has its own integrity. It is not simply material. It exists by God's good favor, and while what is created "may serve humanity," it is so that humanity may "serve God." A mutuality is involved, for the human too is a creature.

The implication for the human, and creation itself, is profound. In a real sense, we are ahead of the story the confession relates. For if the creation

8. Smit, "What Does *Status Confessionis* Mean?"

"awaits the appearance of the children of God," we are talking about salvation and about humanity becoming truly God's children. What happens, and will happen, is a reawakening to the world, not as enchanted, but as more than material. It would be an awakening to the *beauty* of creation, and hence to a mutual sense of delight and wonder. The human is no longer alone; we are drawn not only into mutual communion with one another, but into communion with all creation. Here it might be added that we are beyond a notion of the human as *steward* of creation to the human as sharing in the wonder of creation. Scripture uses the image of the garden both at the outset and at the ending of the canon (Rev 22:1–2). It is a garden that the human is to "till and keep" (Gen 2:15), hence the notion of stewardship. But gardens do not exist simply to produce fruit. The trees of the original garden are not only "good for food" but "a delight to the eyes" (Gen 3:6). Gardens are places of delight, of beauty—to the eye, to the ear, to the nose.

THE HUMAN AS PARTICULAR CREATION

The confession has already noted that the human has a peculiar place in the created order. "All creatures" are created to "serve humanity, in order that humanity may serve God" (art. 12). However, as the confession continues, this has become a problem. Humanity has failed to fulfill its intended task. And worse: it has not just failed through creaturely inability, as though the Creator has required of the human a task that exceeds her ability. The human had, and has, by her own will, turned away from her goal, with disastrous consequences not only for the human, but for all creation. And, furthermore, the human incurs guilt for her action. The human is responsible for the ruination of God's good creation.

Such was not God's creational intention. In one sentence, the Belgic confesses the particular nature of the human creature. On the one hand, God created the human "from the dust of the earth." *Adam*, the name given the human creature, is an intentional correlate of the Hebrew word for "earth," *adamah*. The human being shares materiality, and mortality, not only with all other creatures but with the earth itself. The human is *embodied*. To be human is to *be* embodied. The human is not essentially a spirit or mind that is unfortunately weighed down in a "prison" that grows and degenerates over its short lifespan. We exist as humans with bodies at the will of God! We are not accidents of evolutionary history, even though we may be products of evolution. After all, we emerge from the dust of the earth. Genesis 2 is graphic; humans were molded from clay.

On the other hand, we are made and formed "in the divine image and likeness." This makes the human the peculiar creature that she is. It is "particular," different than all other creatures. A great deal of speculation, both highly sophisticated theological reflection as well as the considerations of "everyday" believers, has surrounded this phrase. Of what, precisely, does that image consist? Is there a certain divine characteristic, perhaps reason or language, that the human shares with the Creator? The confession does not offer a direct answer to that question. Instead, it states the implication: created in the divine image, the human is "good, just and holy: able by the divine will to conform in all things."

Two implications follow. First, since God *creates* the human in God's own image, God *wills* the human to exist. It is *good* for the human to exist. Existence is not a "fall" from perfection. Nor is human existence an accident. Nor is it *as such* a problem.[9] It is God's sovereign good pleasure that we are here, that we exist.

Second, as stated in the previous paragraph, *as such* the human is good, and moreover can be good, that is, can do what the good God wills for the creature. This must be said against the impression often inferred from Reformed thinkers that there is something *fundamentally* wrong with the human, or that we must long to shuck our humanity for something better (this not Reformed so much as heretical). Something has gone wrong for the human, but what has gotten out of kilter is not rooted in the human being as human.

The opening sentence of article 14 sets up the drama for the remainder of the confession: "We believe that God created human beings from the dust of the earth and made and formed them in the divine image and likeness—good, just, and holy; able by the divine will to conform in all things to the will of God." The issue is the rescue of fallen humanity, which constitutes the drama of salvation. This sentence, taken in concert with what is confessed in article 12 on the creation itself, supports the notion that salvation will be the restitution of this lost goodness. Whether salvation is *more* than that is a matter that is to be investigated further within the confession. But that such is *at least* the case appears clear.

9. Van Ruler, "De reformatische visie op de mens," 235.

CONFESSING THE HUMAN

But how can the church *confess* this? That is, how can it claim that it *witnesses* the creation of the human either as creation—the work of God—or that the human is created in the image of this same God? It can claim to do so on the basis of Scripture, to be sure; and in its original context, the Belgic would have held to the Mosaic witness to the creation story. But even a view of Biblical inspiration that holds that God dictated the very words of Scripture to its authors cannot maintain that any *person* witnessed the creation of the human. That would be absurd! One can, however, take the suggestion of Koopmans that the "image of God" can be seen through the lens of the New Testament. There it is Christ who is identified as the image of God.[10] Indeed, he is the "only Son of God" "according to his divine nature" (art. 10). But in the incarnation, he "truly assumed a real human nature" (art. 18). Jesus Christ, then, on the one hand shares our bodily reality, our created nature (and thereby affirms our created, "earthed" nature). But he is at the same time the "image" of God as Son. Without entering the very complex discussion of how this is to be parsed Christologically—what does it mean for Christ to have two natures?—this insight enables us to gain a picture of what true humanity looks like. As we are "conformed" to the image of Christ, we become not less, but more human. And we *can*—or at least the witnesses that put together our New Testament can—give witness to what that looks like. Indeed, through the work of the Holy Spirit, we do in fact see persons who have been conformed to Christ's image. These persons are more fully human as they are drawn into the ways of love and forgiveness, as they exhibit the fruits of the Spirit: love, joy, peace, etc. In this way, we can indicate what God is about with the human.

THE PRIEST OF CREATION

It follows from the preceding that the human has a particular role to play in creation. We have seen that it is in the service of God. But it is more than that. Created in the image of God, the human is a coworker with God in creation. We hear it already in the story of creation from both early narrative reports in the first chapters of Genesis. In the tale from Genesis 1, the newly created humans were told to be "fruitful and multiply," the original command that would reach its climax (or nadir) in the story of

10. Koopmans, *De Nederlandse Geloofbelijdenis*, 70.

Babel. Moreover, they were to "have dominion over . . . every living thing that moves upon the earth" (Gen 1:28). That latter command has been the source of much controversy; has the command to "have dominion" not led to rape of creation by humans as "domination" has become "oppression"?[11] However one reads this, the human was tasked with caring for creation. This is said in a different way in the second creation narrative, where it says that the Lord God put the human in the garden "to till it and keep it" (Gen 2:15).

The human, then, as creature, is responsible to God for the creation. He/she is *response-ible*. The human is a coworker, and as created by the Word the human *responds* to the one who called it into being. This means that the human is, in its essence, *in a particular relation* to God. God addresses, speaks to, calls out the human being. To be human is not simply to be in relation, but in the particular kind of relation that is in essence spoken; it is word and response.

In turn, that makes the human to be the "priest" of creation. That is, from the side of the creature, the human answers God in the name of the creation. The human is the creature with language, the creature that can put the service of God into words, prayer, music. The worship of the church is, then, the heart of the human's task before God on behalf of creation. From the side of God, the human witnesses God to the creation. It does not, note well, take the place of God. It only witnesses to what God is about on behalf of creation: "The creation waits with eager longing for the revealing of the sons of God . . ." (Rom 8:19). Again, the human can do so, can be about this as it conforms to the image of Christ, which is what the human is truly to be about:"Have this mind among yourselves, which you have in Christ Jesus" (Phil 2:5).

REFUSING TO BE HUMAN

I noted above that within God's good creation humans are the problem; they are the problem that drives the drama of salvation history as witnessed in the confession. Moreover, they are the problem because they have willfully turned aside from God's creating intention for the human. Put in theological shorthand, they have *sinned*. Reformed theology and practice

11. The famous Lynn White Jr.'s thesis maintained that the responsibility for the degradation of the environment can be laid at the foot of Gen 1:28. See White, "Historical Roots of Our Ecological Crisis."

have gained the reputation of so emphasizing the sinful nature of the human that one can expect no good from humanity, that humans are fundamentally sinful—read "bad." There may be grounds for that reputation, especially in a practical piety that comes down as hard as it can on the sinful nature of the human so to emphasize the gracious action of God. Against this, however, it must be said that sin is the *second* thing that is said about the human. In fact, while this confession will spend two articles on sin, and will hold nothing back, it encloses the discussion of sin with, on the one hand, the claim that the human is created good and, on the other, with the confession that sin is forgiven. I will argue below that within this context the confession of the sinful nature of the human is *gospel*, good news.

Human sin is not fate. We are not fated to sin because we are created as limited, mortal beings. We said above that to be human exists in responsible relation to God. Sin is the conscious, willful refusal to live in this relation, and hence a refusal to be human, in fact to be ourselves. Sin is a "willing subjection." As the confession puts it, it is "lending their ears to the word of the devil." That, of course, sounds hopelessly outdated, offering the picture of a person with a little creature on the shoulder whispering into an ear. But recall that "principalities and powers" are abroad that beckon us, ask us to listen, offer compelling reasons why we should follow the path of say, conspicuous consumption or violent reprisal against those who do real harm. To whom do we listen? Who "has our ear"? It is whomever we listen to who will offer us safety or comfort or flourishing, so we relate to them and not to God. We expect our humanity to flourish in this other relation. Biblical prophets portray it graphically as an adulterous relationship with one not our spouse (this is perhaps most pointedly put in the first chapters of Hosea).

This is a willful refusal. The human was endowed as good and just, hence as a creature who loves. But love entails the freedom of the will; one wills love. Indeed, because the human is loved, he or she is granted the space, the freedom to choose. The claim of the confession, following Scripture's narrative, is that the human chose wrongly, listening to another who promised human flourishing. In fact, the human often boasts in her freedom. In fact, freedom can become *the* good (it can, in fact become an idol). The result is horror. It is subjection to "death and the curse." The upshot is the *enslavement* of the will: "humans are nothing but the slaves of sin."

The recent film trilogy *The Bourne Saga* nicely illustrates this point. The protagonist, Jason Bourne, is struck with amnesia and spends his time over the three films searching for his own identity. He discovers that he is a killer trained by the CIA. He was programmed to kill, trapped in a deadly profession. When he finally discovers those who have trained him, they remind him that he freely chose to become an assassin. His free choice led to his captivity, a self-imprisonment from which he underwent great effort to liberate himself. The human freely chose to become captive to the power of sin and once captive cannot free himself.

When the confession turns to "original sin" (art. 15), it claims that original sin "has been spread through the whole human race." Moreover, "it is a corruption of all human nature—an inherited depravity which even infects small infants." Something terrible has happened that cannot be undone. Something has gone wrong; what's done is done. We cannot take back what we have done; we cannot undo hurts we have caused. That is evident in our personal lives. But the implications are much broader. The story as it unfolds in the prehistory in Genesis (chs. 3–11) displays how the consequences of the individual act (the original parents) extend far beyond their own deed. In that tale, sin has cosmic proportions.[12] That is the Bible's way of describing a history we know all too well. Sin is not simply about an individual's violation of God's commands, as serious as that is. It is about the horror of violence and refusal to love that issue in repression, hatred, family violence, international terror, the degradation of the earth's environment, etc. Desiring to escape God's rule through the Word, and so to shrug off our essential relation with God, we consequently belong to the kingdom of death.

THE "GOSPEL" OF SIN

As I said above, this is not fate. Van Ruler is helpful here when he notes that the issue with sin is not that it is tragic but that the human is guilty.[13] That is, we are not caught in a fate by which we are compelled to act in such a way that we end up in ruin. Rather, because we have chosen our fate, we bear guilt for the ruination of our lives and our world. It is not fated that nations must live by virtue of violence, or that economies flourish only through inequality. We are not fated to be slaves to whatever desires grab hold of our insides. We are not created as prisoners to the power of what Paul calls the "flesh."

12. Koopman, *De Nederlandse Geloofbelijdenis*, 75.
13. Van Ruler, "De reformatorische visie op the mens," 242.

At first hearing, this does not sound good. This sounds more like giving us all a "guilt complex." Or like the evangelist piling sufficient guilt on the sinner that she flee to Christ as the only refuge for her tormented soul. How can a person live with guilt for what has gone wrong? The answer, of course, is that a person cannot. The weight is too heavy for anyone to bear. How can we survive when we know that it is not simply a matter of individual choices that we make or even the accumulation of choices we have made together? While that may be partly the case, it is not the whole story. For we live in a world shot through with consequences of sin that cannot simply be thought away, or even minimized by managing circumstances.[14] Instead, we employ strategies to avoid responsibility we cannot bear. We deny the consequences. Or we suggest that the human is really good at heart, and so propose that the human *could* and *should* make things better, and so we embark on improvement projects. The problem with such attempts, of course, is that our world doesn't look any better despite all our attempts. And when we are honest with ourselves, the biblical story echoes who we are: we simply run into ourselves and our own willful struggle to free ourselves from our relation with God.

While this is too much to bear, we can be honest because this sin, this "original" sin, is "forgiven by [God's] grace and mercy." We are not trapped. We are not condemned to a Stoic acceptance of fate, to think that the way things are is "the way it is," and so must be, and our best strategy as realists is to make do the best we can. Christian faith is not fatalistic. Evil, for example, is not built into creation. It is not bad to be created. Evil is secondary. Rather, the claim of the confession—and of Scripture—is that the human is taken seriously in his or her own reality. What we do has consequences, and we are responsible. Persons are not pawns of nature and history, but are coworkers with God, and thus of ultimate importance. Hence not only the seriousness of guilt, but moreso the astonishing reality of forgiveness. The world, and the human, is not left to fate. We, and the world, *can be saved*.[15] We can "groan" because we are taken seriously by God.

This is not self-evident. It is not as though we get this simply by opening the morning paper (or reading the home page on our personal computer). We must be told. Because this is about our existence as related to

---

14. Suppose, for example, that we could do something about the racism that infects American history and culture. We still could not reverse time and undo what has been done to those who have suffered the consequences.

15. Van Ruler, "De reformatorsiche visie op de mens," 242.

God, to *this* God, we are addressed by that same God who, in love, tells us that we have chosen to fall out of relation, and so end up in the misery where we find ourselves. "Sin" is an article of faith. It is not about immorality as such, about not being good. In includes that, but by itself it would be about morality. Sin is about our relation—or rather refusal to live in the relation—with God. So God speaks to us, addresses us, for our own good. This is the "gospel" of sin.

CONTEXT II

The confession's theological perspective on the human offers an important and critical witness in an early twenty-first-century world. In the first place, it offers a Christian basis for basic human rights. The language of "rights" as such owes more to Enlightenment thought than to the Christian tradition. The Bible, and even the broad theological tradition, does not make use of the vocabulary of "rights" (even when paired with "duties"). That said, the confession that God wills to create the human in God's own "image and likeness," and so as related to God as God's coworker, lends to every human being fundamental worth. This will be emphasized as the drama of salvation plays out and the Son of God becomes human and goes to the cross to redeem the human. Nonetheless, the human is not valued when saved, but as such, as created in love for God's purpose. That means that the human person is not a cog in an industrial machine, not a statistic on a page, not cannon fodder for humanity's wars, not lost in an anonymous crowd, part of the mass of humanity. This confession alone puts paid to all that humans construct to divide and devalue other human beings.[16]

Secondly, while the value of all human beings is affirmed, the confession enables us to view the world, and ourselves, honestly. There is no need to "prettify" our history, and no claim of moral superiority of one nation or tribe (not even, not especially, a "Christian" tribe). Liberated from the need to justify ourselves, we can[17] look the world squarely in the eye and point out how far short of the kingdom we have come. And we can do so as we own up to our own complicity in the way the world has become. None of this is to deny that good people are at work in history or that God continues to work in and through history—as confessed in the article on providence.

16. On this point see the Belhar Confession, especially para. 4.

17. See what is said aboveabout the creation of the human, and what comes later in the article on sanctification.

Thirdly, together we confess that, valued as we are as individual persons, we live in relation. That primary relation is to God, but through God we become fellow workers with God and one another. To exist, to be, is to be related. This is an important claim given a contemporary, secularized world in which the human has become, in the words of Charles Taylor, a "buffered self."[18] The self, the person, is so set apart from his or her fellow humans—principally so—that she can no longer live in genuine communion. The confession would claim that such is to live under the "curse," for it is to be denied humanity.

Fourth, as God's valued coworker, the human is responsible to God. As one who responds, the human is the addressee of God's command and promise. This means that the human has an active and responsible place within creation and history. And yet this is not to overburden humanity either, as though the human has to do the heavy lifting of saving the world. The confession of original sin makes it clear that the human cannot do so. Rather, that the human exists to "serve God" means that he or she lives in the praise of the Creator and Redeemer. "Yahweh dwells on the praises of his people" (Ps 22:3). God has already effected the salvation of the human and the world. As the confession will go on to claim (art. 24), this frees the human to full responsible action. In the drama of salvation effected by *this* God, the person is liberated to become genuinely human.

18. Taylor, *Secular Age*, 37–42.

5

MESSIAH

ARTICLES 16–21

WE FACE A CRISIS. A crisis is a turning point, a place where the course can go in one direction or another. We are at that point in the confession, at a turning point. But we are at that point because humanity and all creation are at that point. Or so the story of the confession goes and, I will contend, our own story as well.

The crisis is brought on by human sin, sin so pervasive that it envelops all of history and all creation. "Original" sin has caught all of humanity in its net, and has become a power that overwhelms the world's systems. As Genesis 6:11 has it, the earth is "filled with violence." That description is not limited to pre-history but is as present as the newsfeed on our smartphones and as near as our own homes—and hearts. Left to ourselves, we destroy all that is good.

How then, have we survived? The confession offers one answer in the article on providence (art. 13): "We believe that this good God, after creating all things, did not abandon them to chance or future but leads and governs them according to his holy will, in such a way that nothing happens in this world without God's orderly arrangement." The God who is good and the source of all good continues to turn toward this world. But that is not the core of the confession. The core turns around the action that God takes in the person of the Messiah. At the point of crisis, God acts in a decisive, particular, and peculiar way. God so turns to God's creation that the Son becomes incarnate and goes to the cross—the place of crisis—and makes right that which has gone wrong, and for which the human (ourselves!) bears full responsibility.

This, then, is the Christological center of the Belgic Confession. The confession turns on this point. It is here that we witness who God is and what God is about. The gospel has to do with Christ—*sola Christus*. But if this is the Christological center, it is set within a *theological* context. That is, in Christ we not only see what God is about, but what God has intended to be about. What we witness in our own history has its deep root in the nature and reality of God's self. So the confession unfolds. "No one has seen the Father but the Son, and those to whom the Son chooses to show him" (Matt 11:27). In the Son, in the one named Jesus, we catch a glimpse of who God is and hence of God's turn toward God's lost creature—and creation. We are given to see into the heart of God.

ELECTION

That puts us squarely in the doctrine of election. To say that election, or predestination, is a difficult doctrine is an understatement. It has ever been thus. In the seventeenth century, the great Synod of Dort was convened to settle disputes about this doctrine, specifically article 16 of the Belgic. But questions go back to Augustine's dispute with the Pelagians. One can even say that the doctrine of radical grace, which the doctrine of election articulates, reaches back to Scripture; one need only consider Paul's Letter to the Galatians. It is very difficult to discuss today, for the notion that God has chosen the precise number of the saved, prior even to their birth, sounds like a species of determinism, one that ultimately leads to fatalism and with it a sort of quietism or resignation. If all has been determined prior to creation, then of what use is it to do anything, or hope anything? And, in fact, there have been versions of the doctrine that are very difficult to accept, let alone defend. I do not intend to engage such false attempts. Our task is to consider whether and how election can be constituent to a contemporary confession of faith.

It is instructive, then, to follow the confession. It begins by noting that, despite the human predicament and despite human responsibility, God "*showed* himself to be as he is: merciful and just." Moreover, we see this mercy and justice in the person of Jesus Christ. Election, as a doctrine, has its root in Christ—nowhere else: ". . . those who . . . have been elected and chosen in Jesus Christ our Lord." In the person of Jesus, we see that God does not intend for God's children to be destroyed by the ruin they have brought on themselves.

Van Ruler puts it like this. It can be compared to a child who is convinced of the unswerving and unshakeable love of its parents. It is a love that the parents have for the child from before its birth. The child cannot fully understand this; she certainly cannot reason it out. But she lives from that fact. She is free; she can play freely in this world. So to with God. Election is about God's unswerving and unshakeable love.[1] It is about grace. The doctrine of election is a way of talking about the doctrine of grace, which is a way of speaking about God's love.

In fact, one cannot talk about election except after the fact. Too often predestination is placed within or immediately following the doctrine of God, as does, for example, the Westminster Confession. Predestination, *as a doctrine*, discusses whom God will save. But, says Van Ruler among others, election can be considered only retrospectively.[2] It is only as we have been met by Christ, as we have been incorporated into Christ by means of the Spirit, that we can talk about election. It is because at that point we realize that we have not come to where we are by means of our own effort, or even by our own choice, but that this has been God's work.

In this sense, the Reformed emphasis on election is its way of talking of that which the Lutherans indicate by "justification by grace through faith." Justification by grace emphasizes the fact that we flourish before God because we have been made right by God's action, not our own. It is grace. The doctrine of election pushes this back, so to speak, through Christ to the heart of God. We are "chosen in Christ," to be sure, but this fact did not originate historically when the Messiah appeared on the scene but goes back to the heart of God. We were chosen "before the foundation of the world" (Eph 1:4). It is rooted, thus, in the disposition or the will of God. It is an eternal love, a love, that is, that can be neither fully probed nor comprehended.[3] Nevertheless, it is witnessed in Jesus Christ and what he was, and is, about.

This God turns toward this human and turns toward him in the midst of his "physical and spiritual death" (art. 17). God does not abandon the world to its death but enters it, enters to pursue the human. As article 17 puts it so graphically, the human (Adam) flees God, trembling. Humans

---

1. Van Ruler, "Leer van de uitverkiezing," 556–57.

2. Ibid., 564.

3. Noordmans, *Het konikrijk der hemelen*, 102, 107.

live in fear, the confession claims, in fear of God as much as anything. And yet God "set out to find" the human. God's first question to the human in Genesis is "Where are you?" Where have you gone? It is itself a cry of love. And there God meets the human with promise. God promises "to give them his Son, born of a woman, to crush the head of the serpent, and to make them blessed" (Gen 3:15). Whatever one might think of the confession's exegetical take on this text, it clearly wants to claim that from the outset God has pursued the human with promise.[4] And this promise will find fruition in the Son, a Son, it is importantly to be noted, that is "born of a woman." This promise comes in the midst of human suffering and death. The promise at the outset points forward to the situation of crisis.

We might note as well that, as Koopmans adds, evil will not triumph. The promise is that evil will be overcome by the human. The chaos and violence provoked by sin will not have the final word. Nihilism does not have the last say. The human will. However, it is not the human per se, but one particular human, the one "born of a woman," the Son, Jesus Christ.[5]

THE HUMANITY OF THE MESSIAH

The human (we), then, flees God, and engages in her own projects, which results in self-destruction. God, in divine freedom, pursues the human. The Christological center of the confession describes how God takes up the pursuit. It happens in and through Jesus of Nazareth, who meets the human as none other than our brother, God's self in human flesh. We have labeled this as "incarnation," entering the flesh. The eternal Son (the second person of the Trinity) is sent into this world as a human being. As rooted in the Trinitarian reality of God, the incarnation manifests God's turn toward God's creation, particularly the human creature.

In the article on the incarnation, the Belgic emphasizes both that the Messiah is fully human and that he is also the full presence of God's self. Both emphases are present in the testimony of the conception and birth of the Messiah to the virgin Mary. On the one hand, it is made clear that the Messiah is human just like every other human being: he became who he is through the process of cell division, the implantation of a zygote in the womb of a woman, and was birthed like every other human being. He was as vulnerable as any other tiny child then or now. Indeed, he assumed

4. Koopmans, *De Nederlandse Geloofbelijdenis,* 86
5. Ibid.

a "real human nature, with all its weaknesses." The Son of God, then, has entered the reality of our world, with all its pain, terror, and fear—as well as delight, joy, and hope. That means that he was born to a specific woman in a particular place and time in history. He was born as a mortal; he would die.

The confession emphasizes Jesus' location in history when it testifies that this Jesus "descended from David according to the flesh . . . born of a woman; the seed of David; the root of Jesse' descended from Judah, having descended from the Jews according to the flesh; descended from Abraham—having assumed descent from Abraham and Sarah, and was made like his brothers and sisters, yet without sin." He descended "according to the flesh," that is, he came with the same sort of physical genealogy, with ancestors, as all the rest of humanity. But that makes him a particular person with a particular history, of descent from the royal house of David, from the race of Abraham, the patriarch on whose promise Israel rests. This means that God entered human reality as a Jewish Messiah. This is no "general Jesus," no Jesus disassociated from race and culture, from history, a particular history. This Jesus is not the hero of human dreams, a sort of "ideal human," the prototype to which we all might aspire.

Moreover, the confession insists, to enter our humanity is not limited to the assumption of a human body. The incarnation means that that Messiah assumed the fullness of human nature, body and soul. The Messiah did not "ride above" human feelings of sorrow and pain, of temptation and anxiety. The Gospel stories are clear: the Messiah was tempted, felt anguish, underwent not only physical but psychic pain. This defies comprehension indeed. Jesus did not have the kind of knowledge that knew precisely how matters would turn out.[6] But more difficult is the fact that Jesus, as Son of God, does not share in the full knowledge of the divine counsel. Take, for example, Mark 14:32, where the Son knows "neither the day nor the hour" of the coming apocalypse, but "only the Father." It is as though God is in conflict with God's self. That escapes our grasp. And yet the witness is clear that the Messiah was fully human, "all the way down," save for sin—although he was "made sin who knew no sin" (2 Cor 5:21). That is, this Messiah shared in the crisis condition, in the horror of human separation from God with all its consequences. This Messiah himself did not turn against

6. A sort of Sunday school confusion is present with many. They conflate the idea that Jesus is the Son of God with certain divine attributes, in this case the omniscience of God, and conclude that Jesus must know everything that was and is to be. Moreover, this confusion is compounded by filling the notion of omniscience with our own sense of what omniscience must mean!

his Father, did not listen to the voice of the demonic, but nonetheless lived amid the consequence of humanity's rebellion. Indeed, it is much more dire. As Koopmans remarks, in taking on our humanity, Jesus becomes human under the judgment of death. *God* places God's self under the judgment of death. That is to share our humanity to the fullest. That's the point of it all, that God would go this far to rescue a humanity that didn't, and doesn't, wish to be rescued, that flees this pursuing God.

The upshot is that God, as the Son, has become our true companion. The Messiah is our Immanuel, "God with us." Moreover, this one has become our brother at the depth of our humanity, in the waste places of our living. This is the God who is not only present in the wilderness where the oppressed have lost hope as well as protection, in the orphanages that are little more than warehouses for lost children, in the refugee camps where families have lost everything, including their future, in the lonely despair of the battered spouse; this is the God who is present with sinners, those who don't know that they have lost all moral standing in this world. God has "gone to the far country," to echo Karl Barth's sharp observation.[7] "If I make my bed in Sheol, thou art there! If I take the wings of the morning and dwell in the uttermost parts of the sea, even there thy hand shall lead me, and thy right hand shall hold me" (Ps 139:8–9).[8]

But if the incarnation is about the fully humanity of the Messiah, it is that it is *God* who is present in the person of the Messiah. I noted above that the virgin birth emphasized both Jesus' humanity and the fact that God is at work in the incarnation. It is easy to view the virgin birth as a sort of gynecological miracle. But the confession, in conformity with the history of the church's confession of the virgin birth, has to do with the testimony that it is God who is at work already in the conception of the Messiah. That is, it isn't as though God picked Jesus as a virtuous human, worthy to act as God's Messiah. The Messiah is *God* at work, not a cooperative work of God and the human, not even in the conception of this human. Jesus' birth as the Messiah is absolutely God's work.[9] It is, moreover, the sign of

7. Barth, *Church Dogmatics* IV/1, 157.

8. Here we do have an indication of God's attributes, now made manifest in the Messiah. This is God's "omnipresence." It isn't just that God is ubiquitous, rather like the ether, but that wherever one goes there one meets God! We know that because when we have gone to the places where "God can't be" we are confronted by the incarnate Son, the Messiah.

9. The most recent translation of the Belgic includes the unfortunate rendering that the Messiah was conceived "without male participation." The original French can be read

an absolutely *new* beginning. This is not the result of the human project of reconstruction. This is God freely entering human history to be about God's own project.[10]

The article on the incarnation, then, witnesses to the nature of God. *This* is who God is, the one whose Son (fully God) enters human flesh, all the way. We see in this article the anti-docetic witness of the church. That is, this Jesus was not God in human appearance. This is not the Messiah whose flesh or body is unimportant. A more docetic view of Jesus would see in Christianity a religion that represents certain transcendent truths, values even, that come from God. Jesus, from this view, is an exemplary human, one whom we attempt to imitate so to save ourselves from the ruination or dissolution of our humanity. To the extent that contemporary religion exhibits Gnostic tendencies, with its concomitant docetic view of Jesus, the orthodox testimony to a full-bodied incarnation of the Messiah is a startling counterwitness, with its claim that it is God who radically turned to rescue a world in crisis.[11]

ATONEMENT

God's turn toward humanity reached a climax in the incarnation. We are astounded at the wonder that the Son of God took on the full reality of human nature as "God with us" at the depths of human existence. That is not the end of God's "turn," however. It is not just that God has become our companion in the struggles of life. Nor is it the case that in the utterly new reality of the Messiah as God and human a new metaphysical state exists by which humans are enabled to participate in the divine.[12] In the person of the Messiah, God acted in history to meet the crisis, the ruin, into which humanity—and creation—have fallen. God did something that finds its

---

that way, but it actually says that the conception took place without "human" participation. The latter, more accurate translation, makes a much stronger theological claim.

10. Koopmans, *De nederlandse geloofbelijdenis*, 93, 94.

11. See on this Bloom, *American Religion*.

12. The Eastern, or Orthodox, churches would incline more in this direction. For them the problem with humanity is not so much guilt that must be atoned, but weak and transitory human nature that is to be healed. Salvation is not atonement of guilt, but "deification."

climax at the cross. There something took place between God and Jesus, and consequently between God and the human.[13]

Just what that something is is difficult to say. The church has used the shorthand "atonement" to indicate what took place at the cross. But the term does little to report the *what* that took place. It is *that* something happened. Broadly speaking, the church has offered three "theories" of the atonement.[14] The oldest view, sometimes called *Christus victor*, has Christ defeat the powers of sin, death, and evil at the cross. By turning death into an act of love, God triumphs over the powers of darkness. The second, often titled "substitutionary" notion, and deriving from Anselm's famous book *Cur Deus Homo?* (Why did God become human?), is that the human has violated God's justice and so owes God payment. However, since the human is not able to pay the immensity of the debt (and since the debt multiplies every day), Jesus substitutes himself as repayment, thereby satisfying God's justice.[15] A third notion holds that Christ's death is exemplary. At the cross we see the depth of Christ's love and are so moved by his action that we follow, thereby rectifying the human's relation with God. While there are three theories of what happened, broadly speaking, as I said, the theories have a number of variations, thus provoking a continuing conversation on the nature of atonement.

Still, no theory, or better, metaphor, became creedal for the church. However, the second metaphor has received confessional standing in, for example, the Heidelberg Catechism[16] and in part in the Belgic Confession. However, as Colin Gunton claims, the metaphors are not mutually exclusive.[17] In fact, the Belgic speaks of atonement in a variety of ways and does so over a number of articles. Article 19, for example, speaks of Christ's "victory over death," echoing the oldest theory of atonement. In Article 20 the justice of God comes to the fore. In Article 21, dedicated to the atonement, sacrificial images predominant, although they do not exhaust the images present there. And in Article 23, on justification, the confession speaks of sins as "being covered." In his reflection on atonement in the Belgic Confes-

---

13. That the cross is central is evidenced by the amount of space given the passion in all four gospels and the fact that Paul focuses on the cross and resurrection of Jesus—to the near exclusion of discussion of Jesus' life and ministry.

14. Aulén, *Christus Victor*.

15. Hence this theory is also dubbed the "satisfaction" theory.

16. See Q/A 12–18.

17. Gunton, *Actuality of the Atonement*, 83

sion, Verboom follows what he calls the juridical and the cultic aspects of the atonement.[18]

The plurality of images suggests the difficulty in describing just what happened between God and humanity in Jesus at the cross.[19] They also present a danger to the act of confession. It has been easy to transfer the image to the reality, thereby to claim the image or metaphor as the object of confession. But of course we do not, and cannot, confess a metaphor. The metaphor, or better the collation of metaphors, struggles to offer an accurate account of what took place. Metaphors, of course, are not accidental. They manifest a real connection with that which they intend to describe. For that reason, we will take them as offering trustworthy perspectives on the matter at hand. Still, we confess the person, the Messiah, and the fact that he *acted* as such. It is from that action that we reflect on what the confession says about the cross. Nonetheless, the metaphors invite us into that which we confess.

THE JUSTICE OF GOD

The Belgic itself sets the stage for its discussion of the atonement with an article on the "justice and mercy of God." The confession has already spoken of God's justice in its article on election. God is just in that God leaves the sinner to his or her "just" reward. Humanity has "earned" the ruin in which it finds itself. Here, however, divine justice takes a new hue. The justice in view here, however, is *God's* justice: "God has made known his justice toward his Son . . ."

The temptation is to see God's justice as a reflection of our considerations of what counts as justice. We then project that ideal onto God, and measure God's actions against that ideal. It may happen, and does happen, that we get our notion of justice from God's justice; but that is not necessarily so, and given our human penchant to self-justification, even those notions can be easily skewed. This is particularly the case when we take seriously that God makes God's justice known in the Son. For this justice results in the justification of the sinner, something decidedly *not* deserved by the sinner (ourselves!). Hence, God's justice offends our sense of justice!

18. Verboom, *Kostbaar belijden*, 187–91.

19. For her part, Fleming Rutledge identifies eight "biblical motifs" to describe what happens. She acknowledges that eight does not exhaust the scriptural images for what we call "atonement." *Crucifixion*, 208.

Still, the witness of Scripture does not leave us without a sense of what God's justice is about. The entirety of the Old Testament speaks of God's righteousness, or justice, from the establishment of the moral and civic regulations in the Torah, the inclusion of the ceremonial laws designed to re-establish, to make right, the community despite transgressions that resulted in mutual estrangement and distrust, and the declarations from the prophets who spoke for God, demanding justice for the poor and the outcast. Evidently there is a "rightness" to the life of the community that is God's will. It gives place particularly to the oppressed, the left behind, the weak, the broken. God cares, and cares passionately, for God's oppressed children. To violate them is to violate divine justice.[20] Something profound is broken, and humans bear responsibility, guilt, for this brokenness.

That is, God is not indifferent to the horrors of our present age. God is not indifferent to the death camps, to the townships, to the innocent victims of drone attacks, to the children of AIDS, to all the pain that afflicts God's beloved children. And God is not indifferent to those who have perpetrated the horror. In fact, God's justice is manifest *in the fact* that the Son assumes the very human nature in which "disobedience has been committed." This is God's Son fully entering the situation of both the victim and the victimizer! This God is not indifferent but takes on the full pain of humanity.

It is the human (us!) who is "guilty and worthy of damnation"! That will sound too strong for us. We may plead guilty, but not of "crimes against humanity," not of the horror inflicted on God's little ones. We cannot admit to such horror, or at least cannot do so and look ourselves in the mirror. We can confess it (both as confession of faith and as confession of guilt) only as we witness what God is about at the cross. For there we see humanity's full responsibility on display *and* the atonement of that guilt. We only look back on what took place. We do not see the case laid out against humanity. We see Jesus' death and in the horror of it, we see that only *God* could take on the full weight of the horror. *And* that God did! And thereby we can acknowledge that what took place needed restitution.

Something is broken that needs to be righted if life is to go on, if life is to go on with God, and if God is to go on with our life. The oppressed and the oppressor are lost; there is no future. For the oppressor there is also no moral standing. How can this be made right—before God? The answer is that the horror is so deep that only death "within God" can make things right. Only as God bears the pain is there a future. Not because *we* conclude

20. See here the Belhar Confession, para. 4.

that the situation requires this of God, but because *God* in Christ did it! The cry of dereliction from the cross—"My God, why have you forsaken me?" (Matt 27:46)—is the cry of pain from the center of the universe, from God's own self. In that cry, we hear things being made right at cost, the cost of God's own self![21]

SACRIFICE

Within the same metaphorical world, article 21 shifts to sacrificial imagery at the outset: "We believe that Jesus Christ is a high priest forever . . . and that he presented himself in our name before his Father, to appease his Father's wrath with full satisfaction by offering himself on the tree of the cross . . ." This is Christ as both priest and offering (see Hebrews). The imagery is rooted, of course, in Israel's cult. There sacrifice was made on the Day of Atonement, whereby the sacrifice stood in for that which the guilty deserved and thereby reconstituted the broken community and reconciled the transgressors to God (Lev 16). Now, however, the "lamb that was slain" is none other than the Son of God. The requirement for vengeance, the payment for the wrong done, has been taken care of by God! God has placed God's self, as God's Son, on the altar.

This confession claims that this is to "appease" God's wrath! We are easily put off by the notion of God's wrath. Many have been so reared with the idea of God's punitive response to wrongdoing that God has become a sort of avenging moralist. It may be helpful to think of anger as an aspect of love, an expression of passionate care. Scripture is not shy in speaking of God's wrath or anger. It is anger at sin. And it is anger at the sinner who violates God's good creation, and so God's self. Recall that sin is the rending of God's good creation, the destruction of God's beloved. It is as with a parent who sees her child being harmed. She is filled with "wrath," and justifiably so.

God could leave the world to itself, to its self-destruction. We would be left with a kind of nihilism and with its consequences. We have seen such—the Third Reich and the death camps are but one example. Why did God leave such anger aside? We cannot undo the harm that has been done. Still, we see the cross and we hear the Son's cry. And more, we are witness to the resurrection, the victory over the horror. And we say things like

21. Moltmann, *Crucified God*, 244.

"appease" perhaps because we haven't anything else to say. The idea of satisfaction is inadequate only because we don't have any other way to say it.

PURIFICATION

Another shift in metaphor happens when the confession, using biblical imagery, speaks of the "cleansing of our sins." The allusion here is to the Servant Song in Isaiah that reports that "with his bruises we are healed," we are made whole" (Isa 53:5). The image is of illness, of the body out of kilter. When we are estranged from God and neighbor, when *we* are the instruments of that estrangement, we are not well. We are broken as human beings. Only the removal of sin, of what resides within, can make us whole. But what has been done has been done. We cannot undo the harm that we have caused—or our indifference that has itself brought harm.

We are in an impossible situation. And then we aren't! In ritual terms, the blood of sacrifice, the life of another, alone can "cleanse." But in this case there is no other person (or creature), but only this one who bled out, that is, who died. Again, this is a metaphor that grasps at the deeper reality that at the cross something happened with Jesus before God of such nature that we walk away clean!

In all this—in "satisfying justice," in the "substitution," and in the "purification"—we only grasp at, point to, the events of the cross and claim that there all has been made right between God and us, God and God's creation. The upshot is that not only need we do nothing to reconcile ourselves to God, we cannot. This despite the fact that we try to do so over and again. We do everything from making war to building peace to make things right with God and our world. The witness of the confession is that at the cross it has been made right. We witness God's action on the cross and we know that what we are sure is impossible—forgiveness—has happened!

WHO IS THIS MESSIAH?

At the center of a Christian's confession is the testimony concerning the person of Jesus of Nazareth. He is confessed as the Messiah of Israel—Christ. Moreover, he is identified as both divine and human, or more pointedly as "very God of very God" (Nicene Creed) *and* a human being. This was worked out in the fourth and fifth century to arrive at the formula, "one person, two natures." The confession has been moving in this direction as it described God's turn toward creation as the incarnation of the Son. I have delayed reflection on article 19 on the two natures of Christ until we have seen the point of what God was up to in Christ. That is, we approach the person of Jesus, just who he is, from the testimony of what we witnessed that he did. As K. H. Miskotte put it, we don't know the *what* of Jesus; there is only a reflection on him from those who witnessed him.[22] We know Jesus from his work. We proceed from his action to his being.[23] The climax of his work, according to the Belgic, is his atoning death on the cross. Only from there do we ask, who is he?

Our confession reaffirms the old dogma that in the incarnation the "Son has been inseparably united and joined together . . ." and that in this union are "two natures united as a single person" (art. 19). *How* this happens is neither described nor explained. In fact, it raises many questions. How can one person have two natures? How do the natures relate? Of what does the divine nature consist? Or, more abstractly, was there a time when the Son was not in the flesh? And what does that tell us about the nature of the second person? Or about God? Questions multiply. The point, I think, is that the confession *cannot* answer such questions and, by the nature of its genre as testimony, it is not intended to do so. The biblical witness is to what this Jesus was, and is, about. And in that witness we see that this person is both "very God of very God" and human. Since we are astonished because this is a unique event/person, we have no categories, no way to explain what we witness. We can only point.

This is a person with a body like all other bodies. The body has been resurrected, to be sure, but the immortality thereby obtained does not mean that his is a different *sort* of body than ours. Jesus shares in our personhood to such an extent that he dies, spirit and all, his "divinity" going to the grave with him. That is, we meet a person in the same condition as ourselves. But at the same time this person is totally different; this is God fully present with us! There is no explaining, only a pointing, and the necessity to state that this person is both God and human.

Once we have circled around to this claim, the implications are both great and wondrous: "These are the reasons why we confess him to be true God and truly human—true God in order to conquer death by his power, and truly human that he might die for us in the weakness of his flesh." Here we have a hint of the "old" theory of atonement, victory over the powers

22. Miskotte, *De kern van de zaak*, 72.

23. Ibid., 62f.

of death, evil, and sin. In the article on creation, the confession speaks of angels and demons. We noted in that place that such realities persist in our age. We know that the specter of death not only hangs over our lives in the fact that we are mortal; we know death that wields its power in war and oppression, in famine and epidemic, in impoverishment and prejudice. The claim is that this Jesus is such that, as God entering our flesh, as fully God and fully human, he defeats that power. God has turned toward the world to break the back of the power of darkness that causes human misery.

CONTEXT

The problem that atonement attempts to address is narrated in a contemporary setting by Ian McEwan. As a non-believer, McEwan has no interest in presenting or defending Christian notions of atonement. Hence he presents the problem with all the more urgency. In his book of that title, a young girl misinterprets an adult encounter between two older persons, and will falsely identify one of the principals as a rapist. The accusation ruins the lives of both persons. The young girl spends the rest of her life trying to make good, to atone for, that action. As the novel proceeds the two principals find each other and a measure of happiness. It turns out, however, that the reader is reading a tale written by the young girl in later years, a tale intended to atone, to make up for, the "sin" she had committed. The two lovers had, in fact, died early; they had never gotten past the ruin caused. The book concludes:

> The problem these fifty-nine years has been this: How can a novelist achieve atonement when, with her absolute power of deciding outcomes, she is also God? There is no one, no entity or higher form that she can appeal to, or be reconciled with, or that can forgive her. There is nothing outside her. In her imagination she has set the limits and the terms. No atonement for God, or for novelists, even if they are atheists. It was always an impossible task, and that was precisely the point. The attempt was all.[24]

Something has gone wrong for which someone bears responsibility. That wrong cannot be made right. And that, precisely, is the crisis noted at the outset of this chapter. Things have gone wrong, and humans (we) are responsible. It is the scourge of slavery and of racism. It is the reality of

---

24. McEwan, *Atonement*, 350.

poverty. It is the plague of child abuse. It is the numbing violence of wars that keep breaking out. It is environmental degradation that rains death on humans and the planet alike. And we cannot turn the clock back and undo the harm that has been done. Atonement appears to be impossible.

And yet, Christians claim that with Jesus, and particularly with his death and resurrection, they can live forward. Something has taken place that has made things right. And it has to do with Jesus *as well as* with ourselves and the world we inhabit. It goes back to the biblical story, but the biblical story engages the present—so articles 2–7 of this confession. This God's turn toward the world and so to humanity has its origin in the heart of God, a matter that escapes our probing, hence the confession of the doctrine of election. Christians witness that the peace that has grasped them comes from without. It does not have its origin within themselves.

Moreover, this reality has been made real and visible in the person of Jesus of Nazareth, a figure who lived like any other person on earth. We can only witness, or point to, that person and confess that in him we are confronted with one who is both God and human. We have no categories by which to classify this person; we are astonished by the stories, and more, we are startled by his presence.

Jesus fascinates and puzzles, and does so for many beyond Christianity. Indeed, Jesus continues to fascinate two millennia following his death. We might ask, why? Is he simply a compelling figure? Does his portrayal evoke deep human needs and longings? Do contemporaries perceive something more about Jesus than might adhere to other, even saintly figures from world history? At the least, interest in Jesus indicates a deep longing for rescue from ruin, whether within persons, or in the social-political reality of the world in crisis.

In that context, Christians claim that in this person God has—as human person!—plumbed the depth of human existence, has shared with us the horror and pain of this life. And more, that God has taken on God's self the responsibility, or blame, or guilt, if you will, that rightly belongs to us humans, individually and collectively, has born the horror within God's self. For the horror of the dying of the innocent, the horror of the evil perpetrated by humans, is so great that only a death so great that it can only be hinted at by the "death of God" can bear it. With stammering and inadequate metaphors, Christians point to the cross, the execution of this Jesus who is none other than God's self manifesting a love that has its origin in the heart of God (election).

6

THE RESCUE OF THE HUMAN
ARTICLES 22–26

IN THE INTRODUCTION, I indicated that the first articles of the confession set the faith firmly within the common Christian tradition. Despite some nuances (I think particularly of the articles on Scripture), the confession can be said to do just that up through the article on the atonement. With article 22, we see a shift to more Reformational themes: faith, justification, and sanctification. Not that those themes were absent from the church's thinking prior to the Reformation. That would hardly be the case. But the Reformers were clear that they understood these themes quite differently, a difference that would result in the tragic rendering of the unity of the church. The Reformers *witnessed* God's work with the human differently than their Roman Catholic counterparts. It is here that the radical doctrine of grace takes hold, albeit that grace itself does not emerge as an explicit theme. But the doctrine of justification by grace through faith rests on the sovereign freedom of God's turn toward the human in love. Any notion that human effort can in any measure participate in "obtaining" a right relation with God, apart from which the human has no hope, is rejected.

The turn taken at article 22 is signaled with the question put at the outset of that article: How can we know what God was about in Christ in bringing about the atonement of the human caught in the crisis of human sin? The confession offers an answer at the outset of article 22—"the Holy Spirit kindles in our hearts a true faith"—but it has already provided an answer earlier in the confession in its discussion of the authority of Scripture (art. 5) and the claim that we believe what is contained in Scripture "because the Holy Spirit testifies in our hearts that they are from God." We could say, then, that the confession shifts thematically to the Spirit as it turns to the "righteousness of faith" and the "justification of sinners."[1]

Furthermore, we see the Trinitarian nature of God as a continuing theme in the confession in this turn to the believer. The confession is witness of God's action in history. It is *this particular* God who turns toward creation and the human, whose Son has become incarnate and who goes to the cross for the sake of a humanity that persists in turning against God. It is *this particular* God who is present in the Holy Spirit as the Spirit wakens within us a confidence in the free turn of God, historically present at Golgotha.

As we saw in the previous chapter, at issue is how we can be right with God. This is crucial if it is of the essence of the human being how she stands in relation to God.[2] To be human is to live in relation, and the primary relation is to the creator. That relation, however, has been broken (art. 14). In fact, the human lives with the reality of guilt, the very real and objective responsibility for the ruination of God's good creation, including not least of all the ruination of a person's relation to the God who loved her into existence. That guilt impedes a full relationship. Justification is liberation.[3] "I am now free from guilt. Thereby I come to stand in a space: I can exist in the presence of God and all humans; I can exist in the judgment of God."[4] The confession dedicates two articles to these themes: article 22 concerns the *ground* of justification and article 23 concerns the *essence* of justification.

I BELIEVE

The slogan "justification by faith" is misleading. It can easily be understood as the claim that we do something—commit the act of believing—that

---

1. In this it is only following the Apostles' Creed, and for that matter John Calvin, who places these themes in book III of the *Institutes*, where "the way in which we receive the grace of Christ" is described in terms of the work of the Spirit. This also puts paid to an oft-heard complaint that the Reformation either ignored or underemphasized the work of the Holy Spirit.

2. VanRuler, "De iustificatione," 164.

3. Verboom calls it "liberation in *optima forma*." *Kostbaar belijdenis*, 219.

4. Van Ruler, "Rechtvaardiging," 160.

merits a counteraction by God, who thereby restores us to right relation. In that instance, faith is to conceive of something as true that cannot be proven to be true, often something particularly difficult. It is contrasted with knowledge. I cannot *know* that Jesus Christ was born of Mary, but I can *believe* it. Belief is a lower order of knowing. But the Reformers never intended faith to be understood as an action that gains divine favor: "we do not mean, properly speaking, that it is faith by itself that justifies us."

Faith on that account easily becomes a theme in itself. That is, we consider a "person of faith" to be someone who is open to that which transcends what our empirical world presents. One has "faith" in the transcendent. Someone of "another faith" is an adherent to a different religion. She or he believes in "something more." We value such faith positively. But that is not what the confession intends when it speaks of faith. One of the slogans of the Reformation was "faith alone." However, it was not, and is not, a matter of simply having faith that is at issue. The question is the *content* of faith. What, or who, is it that one has faith *in*? As T. F. Torrance put it, "Faith is thus a polar concept that reposes upon and derives from the prior faithfulness of God which has been translated permanently into our actual human existence in Jesus Christ."[5] The consequence is that "we look away from ourselves altogether . . ."[6] We do not look to whether we can "suspend disbelief" concerning "religious matters." It is not about our ability to do anything.

It is about the *content* or object of faith. That is, it is about Jesus Christ and of what Christ is about. It is about the God revealed in Christ, and so, as we have seen, about this particular God who has turned toward God's creation. We *discover* that we believe. Indeed, we *witness* to that discovery, in this instance, a witness to something that has happened to ourselves and within ourselves. In this discovery, we point "away from ourselves altogether." It is the Holy Spirit who "kindles in our hearts a true faith," or confidence in the report that has reached us, a report concerning the object, Jesus Christ, such that we "embrace" him. The Heidelberg Catechism (Q/A 65) describes how this happens: "The Holy Spirit produces [faith] in our hearts by the preaching of the holy gospel, and confirms it by the use of the holy sacraments." It is in *hearing* the voice of the One who addresses us in proclamation[7] that we are wakened to a story that so captures us that

5. Torrance, *Theology in Reconstruction*, 159.

6. Ibid., 161.

7. One could say that this is Scripture, but it is in fact the Word proclaimed, which

we give it our full trust. We have heard God's own self, and we can but give this God our full trust. But again, it is not simply trust itself, it is trust *in* the One to whom God testifies, God's own Son, Jesus Christ.

A pair of stories from the Synoptic Gospels can be of assistance here. A desperate woman is at the center of both tales. The one is about a Gentile woman whose daughter is demon possessed (Matt 15:21–28). Jesus refuses her request for healing by responding that he "was sent only to the lost sheep of the house of Israel." And if that weren't enough, Jesus tells her that "it isn't fair to take the children's bread and throw it to the dogs." The woman abases herself by answering that "even the dogs eat the crumbs that fall from the master's table." At that point, Jesus exclaims, "Great is your faith!" The second story is of a woman ill from a menstruation that doesn't cease (Mark 5:25–34). The woman spies Jesus among a crowd and, hesitant to approach him directly, desires only to touch his garment. She does so and is healed. Aware that the woman has been healed, Jesus remarks, "Daughter, your faith has made you well."

What is "faith" about in this pair of tales? It surely is not adherence to an established doctrine about who Jesus is—the son of God, or somesuch. At first glance it appears to be an internal act of the will, a trust that this Jesus can heal. Something like that may have been present; certainly there were faith healers about in whom followers placed their confidence or trust. It *is* focused outward, on an object/person. But it is almost a negative, a desperation, coming with nothing but need, a need deep enough to step aside from all self-regard. It is a certain emptiness, a lack, a humility before this other, this stranger, Jesus. Faith is "only the instrument" by which we "embrace Christ" (the content or object of faith). Faith could be compared to perceptual capabilities. We see through eyes. The eye is not the object of sight; the eye receives the imprint of the object (through nerves, brain, etc.). We are given sight; it comes (or not) with birth as a human. It is an instrument of reception, as it were. Faith is that open place, that space where we set down the effort to achieve, and receive—perhaps in desperation, perhaps because we have nothing else.

In any case, it is a gift. The "Holy Spirit kindles [sparks] it in our hearts." The confession *witnesses* here. The believer acknowledges that the God who engages history has engaged her very self, as a space is opened within herself that points her beyond herself to know that her "entire salvation," the presence and future of her humanity, is in the person of Christ.

---

is based on Scripture, but it is not confined to the written Word.

She acknowledges that she has not achieved this trust by dint of her own effort, by investigation or through religious practice, but that it comes as gift.

IN RIGHT RELATION

It is sometimes difficult to discuss faith as a separate theme because we then turn to ourselves and the quality of our faith—Do we have enough? Are we truly faith-ful in our lives?—and we pay a great deal of attention to our inner life and our individual relation to God. Such attention is not to be disregarded. God's turn toward creation is a turn toward the human, the human as individual person. And the Reformation heritage has spawned movements that concentrate on God's relation to the individual in his or her internal life. Such is the case with Pietism, for example, or the "further Reformation" that would emerge in the Netherlands in the century following the writing of the Belgic Confession. Still, this confession's discussion of faith points away from the individual to the object, to Christ. It *includes* the individual. But it is clear that the right relation obtained is not in us, but in Christ. "Jesus Christ is our righteousness." The rightness I have with God is mine only to the extent that it has been obtained for me in Christ, and my identity with God is in this Other.

The trajectory of the confession leads to this point. From the nature of God—who is good and the source of all goodness, and who is in God's self triune—the confession traces God's action and presence to the Son's incarnation, thereby taking on our humanity, and atonement, thereby reconciling us to God in the historical action of the cross. This Christ, the Messiah of Israel, is the one in whom my relation with God has been re-established. Can one even say, in this context, with Torrance that the relationship that is described as "faith" is not in ourselves but in Jesus, the one who takes our humanity within his own: "We do not rely . . . upon our act of faith, but upon the faith of Christ which undergirds and upholds our faith"?[8] A reading of Romans 3:22 would support that claim, where the "righteousness of God" was manifested "through the faith of Jesus Christ."[9]

This, then, is justification. The right relation has been established through the action of Jesus Christ. There is something startling about this, even scandalous. It makes no sense that the *sinner* is justified ("while we were yet sinners, Christ died for us," Rom 5:8). The sinner turns away from

8. Torrance, *Theology in Reconstruction*, 159.
9. Reading the construction of the sentence as a subjective genitive.

right relation—with God and his or her neighbor. That's the nature of sin. We posit ourselves, live independently. In fact, the sinner—that's every one of us—seeks to justify himself or herself. It is simply not possible then for the sinner to be justified. The testimony of the apostles before the council sharpens this astonishing claim. The one whom "you killed" is exalted "to give repentance to Israel and forgiveness of sins" (Acts 5:30, 31). Those who kill the one who is God present are the very ones, Israel, for whom this one dies for their forgiveness!

And yet, the sinner is "declared" right. The context of the Reformation is important here. The Reformers were tilting against the established church's notion that in justification the sinner was *made* right. That is, that God works with the sinful human so that she *becomes* a righteous person, loving, obedient, and so on. In contrast, the Reformers insisted that the sinner was *declared* right.[10] It isn't as though a change needs to take place with the person before she can be in right relation with God, and so claim her place in life and history. The rightness is there for her already in Christ's action. So she is welcomed by God *as a sinner*. This is not to validate her sin, nor to take the edge off her enmity to God. It is the sheer mercy of the God who turns toward the broken human that allows her to come with empty hands and empty heart, as one "poor in spirit."

We come because the very real guilt that obtains to us all has been removed. Through Christ's action our sin has been forgiven. While the confession does not make of this a separate theme, forgiveness is central to justification. When Christ's "benefits are made ours, they are more than enough to absolve us of our sins" (art. 22). And, Christ's obedience is "enough to cover all our sins" (art. 23). The impossible has happened; what had been done, what had taken place, no longer obtains. That which disrupts our right relation has been either "absolved" or "covered." Salvation is a sort of negative: it *removes* that which hinders our right relation with God and our neighbor.

In this event, our humanity is respected by God in that we are esteemed as responsible, as mature humans. But in our responsibility, we have turned against God, the result of which is a blood-stained world, torn apart in violence and prejudice. Indeed, as we saw, at the heart of it all is our insistence on our own way. So long as the guilt remains, there is no reconciliation, no "right relation." It is the stunning reality of the cross, where God takes on all the responsibility, all the pain, all the ruin, onto God's self. Only now do we

10. Koopmans, *De Nederlandse Geloofbelijdenis*, 112.

stand within that impossible, even scandalous, morally repugnant situation where the sinner—ourselves—is justified, given a place.

The upshot is the recovery of our lost humanity. We "recognize ourselves as we are" (art. 23). There is humility in this. This is not a false humility, a denigration of the gifts and accomplishments that we enjoy. It is, rather, to acknowledge that our worth as humans, our place, does not rest on anything that we do. The upshot of this is quite startling. *We* don't have to accomplish anything to find meaning and hope. That has already taken place. Van Ruler asks, "Why must everything have a cause and reason, a goal and meaning, a use? God and only God, God's self *is* the justification of all created things."[11] With that assurance we can relax. This "makes us confident." Our conscience is free "from the fear, dread, and terror of God's approach . . ." (art. 23). As a result we can play. We can delight in the wonder of God's created reality. We can live. We can be human.

MADE NEW

I noted above that the gospel discovered by the Reformers was that we are made right with God without being first changed into the kind of persons who would qualify for God's favor, but that justification is of the sinner who comes with nothing in hand. That is not to say that the Reformers were disinterested in the Spirit's work in remaking or reorienting the sinful creature. While it is indeed true that "God grants righteousness apart from works" (art. 23), that does not mean that human action is unimportant or irrelevant. The confession dedicates an article to the "sanctification of sinners" in which the church confesses that "we do not wish to deny that God rewards good works." Works do not count for salvation—"we do not base our salvation on them"—but works still count!

But how do we get to that point? It is, says the confession, that "this true faith . . . regenerates us and makes us new creatures." We are remade through faith! "This true faith" carries forward the previous article, which we have now understood as a profound openness to that which is beyond ourselves, as we look to Christ. It is in this open or empty space that the new is born. Koopmans puts it like this: "Without faith in justification there is no true knowledge of the love of God and also no action that emerges from the love of God, but only self-love or fear."[12] We cannot know that we

11. Van Ruler, "De iustificatione," 190.

12. Koopmans, *De Nederlandse Geloofbelijdenis*, 119.

are already loved, valued, and so of worth to God. Without that knowledge we are left with ethics. That is, we are left finding the right way to be and to act in the world. At heart, it is self-preservation, egoism. Put another way, it is the anxious quest to obtain justification on our own. But to know one is loved is to be freed from that need. Our work is the fruit of justification. But it is the fruit of justification because through justification the Spirit makes us new.

Works count; the good God cares for creation and for the human in creation. So of course works are important, and important to God. Works have to do with how we are human together, with the ethos of living. Indeed the Torah was God's gift to God's people as it guided them in how they could live their lives. The Torah is not an antiquated piece of writing, or left to Israel. It is part and parcel of "God's revealed Word in writing . . ." (art. 3). With that in mind, we read the confession's article on sanctification as the Spirit so engaging us in God's work that we share in God's purpose for humanity. At the same time, *we* are regenerate as we become fully part of God's action in creation and with our sisters and brothers.

We see, then, a dynamic movement within the confession. God is "going somewhere." It is not as though we have been justified and that settles matters. It is not that we have been saved for a future blessedness. God has plans for the creation. As Van Ruler trenchantly puts it, everything "turns about justification," but it is not "all about justification."[13] Justification is not the goal, it is the means to the goal, which, Van Ruler claims, is the kingdom of God.

This is further set out in what to contemporary readers might appear as a rather odd article in the confession on the "fulfillment of the law" (art. 25). De Brès set it in just the right place here. For it both summarizes what the Messiah was about in history and indicates what works are about for the believer, justified and regenerate.

The confession distinguishes the ceremonial laws of the Torah from what we call the "moral" laws. Ceremonial laws, having to do with the liturgical life of Israel, are fulfilled in Christ. Hence their use "ought to be abolished among Christians." The fulfillment, however, is crucial. What they intended—the restoration of community through the system of sacrifices—has been obtained in Christ's death as a sacrificial offering on behalf of the human. It is for that reason that we read the ceremonial laws, not simply out of curiosity, and certainly not to repeat them, but to understand

---

13. Van Ruler, "De iusitifactione," 169.

what God was about in Christ's death. We confess in his death the permanent removal of sin, a priestly act that, given the identity of the priest (and victim)—Christ—need not be repeated. Justification in the forgiveness of sins is a completed act. It is a done deal. We do not have to work to attain it; our work in this case being concerned to offer proper obeisance to God.

But the second part of article 25 is crucial in this context. The "law and the prophets" remain witnesses that "confirm us in the gospel" and "regulate our lives with full integrity for the glory of God, according to the will of God." Here the dynamic nature of God's history with creation is fully focused. The mention of "law and the prophets" is notable. It is easy to understand this article from the perspective of the individual: this is how *I* as a child of God act now that I am free to love. This impression is reinforced by the Heidelberg Catechism when it discusses the law in the third part of that document. In that context, the catechism views the law as a means by which believers express their gratitude. And the "law" part of that section focuses on the Ten Commandments. Hence, I guide my life by that handy, well-known set of regulations. But the Belgic points to the entire law and prophets, which is a guide for *Israel*, a people. Moreover, the law and the prophets indicate God's intention for a new kind of community, where we read regulations concerning wealth and poverty, war and peace, family life, violence against the helpless, use of the land, and so forth.

K. H. Miskotte writes of what he calls the "surplus" of the Old Testament.[14] There are, he says, promises in the Old Testament that have yet to be fulfilled. The coming of the Messiah fulfills the promise, but does not complete it. So, we can say, the full coming of the reign of God that is imaged in places like Isaiah 65 (where "no more shall there be in it an infant that lives but a few days, or an old man who does not fill out his days" and "the wolf and the lamb shall lie down together . . .") has not yet happened. The Messiah has come to inaugurate that kingdom, but it has only begun. It is "already and not yet." The believer, freed in justification and regenerate by the Spirit, can read out God's intention from the "Word written down" and can act accordingly. Not by force, and not because in so doing he or she will win God's favor, but because he or she is taken up in a life for the glory of God—which is to extend forward to what this good God has intended for creation from the outset.

We see this dynamic embodied in a vignette from Acts:

---

14. Miskotte, *When the Gods Are Silent*, 173–302

> Now the company of those who believed were of one heart and soul, and no one said that any of the things which he possessed was his own, but that had everything in common. And with great power the apostles gave their testimony to the resurrection of the Lord Jesus, and great grace was upon them all. There was not a needy person among them, for as many as were possessors of lands or houses sold them, and brought the proceeds of what was sold and laid it at the apostles' feet; and distribution was made to each as any had need. (4:32–25)

Freed from their need to justify themselves, the community engaged in a new way of being in the world. They did so freely. In so doing, the beloved community began to take shape. The community became a prefiguration of the kingdom of God, a "firstfruit" (Jas 1:18).

COMMUNION WITH GOD

This section of the confession rounds off with a long article on the "intercession of Christ." More than many other articles, this emerges from its particular historical context. When the Belgic was written, religious life of its era was filled with saints and images, processions and devotions, all designed to assist the pious believer in his or her relation with God. The saints functioned not only as examples of holy living, but could act as intercessors with God. The believer could pray through them; they merited a place in heaven and hence had access to the throne of God. The saints, particularly Mary, were granted that status because not only was God distant, but God's Son was a distant and frightening figure as well. The believer needed one who understood the frailties and failures of human existence, and so could plead with God out of understanding.

The confession builds on the earlier articles that have to do with Christ and his work. He is not distant and need not be feared. The Son who "assumed our nature" was sent by the God who is "merciful" (art. 20). He is the one who went to the cross, the one who died for our sins, who is the judge. Moreover, he knows us, having been tempted as we have, having suffered as we do. With Christ as our intercessor, then, we have *already* obtained a place with God through the one who is our "rightness."

CONTEXT

If the confession was written against the question of how one obtains access to the mercy of God, to what extent does that apply in our current situation? Does justification by faith respond to the concerns of the contemporary persons, religious or otherwise? It might appear at first glance that the issues forefront in this chapter are antiquated, a concern of earlier generations. The secular person doesn't even consider God as he or she goes about her business of finding her way in life. There is no threat of divine condemnation. Nor is there promise of communion with the God present in Scripture.

But if the context has changed, has the deep need to be justified disappeared? And if it is not the God of Scripture present at the boundaries of history and humanity, then there are ersatz "gods" aplenty who lurk and demand our obeisance as payment for justifying our existence. Eugen Rosenstock-Huessy put it like this a little more than a half a century ago: ". . . man [sic] is divided from animal nature by the one fact that any group, nation, tribe, member, human individual, wherever we find him is occupied in justifying himself to himself, to others, and to the kind."[15] We do so by conforming to the "laws" laid down by the "gods." We follow the gods of commerce, and so exhaust ourselves so that we can purchase that which displays our worth, or can find our place in the economic system, and so be justified by the work we do, the career we achieve. We follow the gods of Cupid and Eros, and find our worth in loving relationship. The god of war beckons us, and we are justified as we become belligerent. Tribes, ethnic enclaves, long for validation, and so conform to an ideal. We attempt to justify ourselves by the work that we do.

And so we are enslaved to a system of "law" every bit as confining as a religious legalism that requires that we observe its prescriptions and proscriptions in order to find peace with God. That enslavement exhausts us as it requires all our time, our energy, our money, and even our children! Only so, we think, can we claim worth as humans, and only so can we be justified in taking up the space we do in community, society, and even on planet Earth.

In this context, the Pauline message of justification is indeed "liberation theology in optima forma."[16] The gospel is one of freedom. John Calvin

---

15. Rosenstock-Hussey, *Speech and Reality*, 74.

16. Verboom, *Kostbaar belijdenis*, 219.

speaks of freedom as, first of all, freedom from enslavement to the law.[17] Van Ruler says somewhere that freedom is the essence of being. Human sin is that we desire to escape what we are, creatures. Acting on that desire, we lose our freedom. Salvation is Jesus' "yes" to the creature, and that "thereby we are liberated to accept ourselves fully and the fact that we exist."[18] We need no longer kill ourselves—and one another—in validating and justifying our existence. Our justification has already taken place in Christ. Our worth, our rightness in the world, is external to us, but involves us. We are, literally, eccentric.

This freedom plays itself out in a variety of ways. Because we are free from the need to justify ourselves, we can allow others *their* freedom. I do not need the other to conform to my understanding of how one is to be in the world and thereby release me from my own anxieties that perhaps I have it wrong. I can allow the other his or her place. Nor is this a matter of individuals, a sort of tolerance for those different than myself. This is a social reality. As free people, we can allow others their own freedom. In this way, justification is the theological basis for human rights. The language of rights is not, in itself, Christian. We have built the notion of rights on the foundation of creation: "all men are created equal." And the biblical warrant, of course, can be found in Genesis, where the human is created "in the image and likeness of God," or in such statements like, "God shows no partiality." That is true enough. But it is also true that Christ died not only for myself and for my kind, but for the sinner, for the ungodly. And *as such* he, she, they are fully deserving of the respect for their freedom.

In this context, freedom also means that I am free to be changed, challenged, drawn into a new way of being, in a new community of others. I need not construct protection for my vulnerable "self." My self already exists in Christ, in the presence of God. Hence the other can change and challenge me. Justified, I am engaged in God's justice, as the Belhar Confession has it. My way of being, and the way of being of my tribe in the world, may need to give way in order that God's justice for the weak, for the oppressed, for the broken can burst forth—and I and my kind not only have not lost anything, but we have gained in a new communion, one built not on the systems of justice (and justification) that we have constructed, but on one instituted in Christ and effected in the Spirit.

17. Calvin, *Institutes*, III.19.
18. Van Ruler, *Een leven een feest*, 139.

Freedom, moreover, is expressed in work and in play. We no longer work to guarantee our place in the valuation by self or society. We work with great energy because we are free to do, now, that which enhances the flourishing of our fellow humans and God's good creation. And we are free to play, simply to be, to delight in beauty and wonder, to engage in that which has no purpose, no goal beyond the doing—which is what art does at its purest, but not only art; sport does so as well, as does the play of the enjoyment of, say, hobbies.

This freedom finds its fullest expression in worship. "Praise," says Van Ruler, "is the only adequate response to the creative action of God."[19] We are most human when we praise, when we sing together in honor of God. We fulfill the law of God, freely, and so "regulate our lives with full integrity, to the glory of God . . ." Worship is, then, the full expression of human freedom in the face of the gods of the age that would demand our allegiance. Worship is testimony to this God, and what this God is about.

WITNESS

In this context, our confession witnesses to God's action on behalf of the human in justifying and sanctifying her. We point to what God has done. On the one hand, the church tells Scripture's story, which is itself historical witness of those who know the freedom to live fully in God's presence, and so to live fully in the world. This witness is not *our* experience, but it is the experience of the community, handed on through the generations. Today we say, "This happened." And so it is a witness to a history.

But it is not only that. It is witness that the church makes today. It is to observe the freedom that our sisters and brothers know, and that we know as well, a freedom that we know does not emerge from ourselves, from our own effort, from our own doing. It is not a freedom earned, but a freedom received. We learned that the force, or energy, or liberation comes from God present and at work in the Spirit. We observe that we do believe, and that in that faith we are set free. We cannot prove this. We testify to it. And in that testimony is our freedom.

19. Ibid., 139.

7

THE COMMUNITY OF FAITH

ARTICLES 27–32

THE CONFESSION TAKES ANOTHER turn beginning with article 27. The next nine articles—nearly one quarter of the entire confession—deal with the church. The sacraments will be discussed in the following chapter. The most obvious shift is from God's engagement with persons, an engagement that comes to climax in the intercession of the ascended Christ, to the community of faith, believers together. God's turn toward creation now finds expression in the reality of the church.

The emphasis on the church is in large part explicable from the context of its writing. The church itself was at issue in the turbulent time that we would later call the Reformation.[1] Indeed, this confession was written in large part to claim legitimacy for those who had taken the new course. De Brès and his compatriots were not arguing for an alternate way of being Christian; they were claiming that they remained in the "true" church, indeed, that they were part of the "one" church, as we shall see. But what *is* this church? Their response describes a church quite different than the established Roman church.[2]

---

1. The history of the Reformation and the issues involved are, of course, too large and complex a topic to undertake in this essay. A vast literature exists that recounts the events and issues of the Reformation.

2. Although it could claim to be consistent with ways in which, e.g., Augustine and Cyprian viewed the church. See Calvin, *Institutes*, IV.

Moreover, as I noted in the introduction, this portion of the confession expresses a particularly *Reformed* understanding of the church. As the Belgic has it, this church takes a different shape than do the Lutheran churches on the one hand and the Anabaptist expressions of the faith on the other. The Belgic will go on to confess that the church has certain office-bearers and a means of governance that give expression to the true nature of the church. We will discuss this particularity below.

There is still another shift present at the turn to article 27, this of a theological nature. Article 26 brings to a climax the discussion of God's action in Christ in justifying and sanctifying the believer, as Christ mediates with the Father on behalf of the believer. As article 27 opens, we are no longer in heaven, but back on earth, with the messy and difficult reality that is the church. However, the church is the *means* by which God, in the Spirit, acts or communicates God's salvific action. Here, of course, one must be careful, as the confession will be. For at issue was whether the church held a monopoly on the means of salvation or could even, as means, effect salvation. Was grace a "something" that could be parceled out to believers through the action of those authorized by the church to do so? If not, that is, if God is not bound, but acts freely with the human, why then church? Is it more, or other, than a collection of the religiously like-minded? The Belgic's answer is a resounding no. But what does it say?

AN IMPOVERISHED COMMUNITY

The Belgic opens its confession of the church with its testimony to "one single catholic or universal church—a holy congregation and gathering of true Christian believers, awaiting their entire salvation in Jesus Christ, being washed by his blood, and sanctified and sealed by the Holy Spirit." Three matters are to be noted: the church as congregation, the expectation of salvation, and how the believers stand in the presence of God and the world.

The church is, first of all, a congregation, or community, or a "gathering."[3] That is to say, the church cannot be understood clerically, as though the hierarchy of the church *is* the church. The offices of the church will find expression in this confession, and they are important (they are,

---

3. Cf. the Heidelberg Catechism 54, where it is the *gemeinde*, or community/congregation. As the *Nederlands Belijdenis* (as the Belgic is otherwise named), the word is *vergadering*.

after all, confessional!). But they *serve* the community, or the gathering of believers. This does not claim that the institution of the church is somehow *not* church, but it cannot be understood as exclusively church. There is an anti-triumphal strain here. But it is picked up as we move to the second and third matters emphasized in the opening sentence of the Belgic's confession of the church, present already in the designation of the church as gathering of *believers*.

We noted in the discussion of faith above that faith is an attitude of radical openness. The believer has nothing to offer but her poverty. She is justified only in the work of the Messiah, present to God in the mediation of the ascended Messiah. The community, the church, then, is not a compact of those who bring wealth to a body, who gain strength in numbers, not a movement or party that engages the world on the strength of its religious possession. Rather, believers are gathered in their lack, but a lack that includes the delightful assurance that they are maintained by God in Christ through the Spirit.

This position is further reinforced by the claim that they *await* their full salvation. The church does not *possess* salvation. It is not that something vital and crucial has not happened (see below), but that the fullness of what God is about is not completed. This gives this community an eschatological character. The church cannot claim to be the full realization of what God intends for the world. It can only confess that God is about something with it, something that awaits its completion. The church, then, is not a collection of the satisfied, of the winners in a world of competitive religions. It is those who are gathered under the cry of need. It is as the slaves who cried out in Egypt, whose voice YHWH heard (Exod 3:7).

Still—and this is the third matter—a crucial event has happened that has changed everything. It is as God's turn toward creation found its focal point at the cross. The believers *are being* washed by Christ's blood and are sanctified and sealed by the Holy Spirit. They have not been abandoned to their own fate, left to the hell of existence. The awful events in which death overtakes God's beloved Son have shifted the relation of the believers to God and the world. They can stand with confidence and can engage the world because they have a secure place. Given that this happened through Christ's blood, this is not an occasion for pride. The believer cannot separate himself or herself from the run of humanity, now in happy possession of a solid religious treasure. The believer is incorporated into a community of those who rest their hope, their identity, themselves on the one who died for them, and are maintained in the relationship by God's own self in the power of God's Spirit.

The church, then, is an impoverished community. It is unique in the world because it has nothing to offer.[4] That reality manifests the Lutheran claim that the doctrine of justification is the heart of the church. Believers are gathered as those who are justified, who of themselves have nothing to offer, but who are given a community in which they can be fully human, welcomed into communion with God and hence with others. The equivalent Reformed doctrine is election. As we saw, election is a way of talking of the radical grace or love of God, a grace that we did not and cannot earn, but can only receive. Israel's way of expressing this is apt here: "For you are a people holy to the Lord your God; the Lord your God has chosen you to be a people for his own possession, out of all the peoples that are on the face of the earth. It was not because you were more in number than any other people that the Lord set his love upon you and chose you, for you were the fewest of all peoples" (Deut 7:6–7). But it this people that is called to be the church. Or as Koopmans has it, "the church is the place where Christ chooses to dwell together with sinners."[5]

By noting that God chose Israel, or that Christ chooses to dwell with us poor sinners, we signal that this impoverished community did not form itself. It is not a gathering of the religiously like-minded, or a collection of those who chose God. It is not constituted by itself, certainly not on the strength of a certain quality of the faith of its members, not from a position of organizational or financial or societal strength. We will comment further on the "marks" of the church below. However, article 29 is clear that the true church is recognized in the "pure preaching of the gospel" and the "pure administration of the sacraments."[6] As the Heidelberg 54 has it, "The Son of God, through his Spirit and Word . . . gathers, protects and preserves for himself a community . . ." The community exists by virtue of Christ's presence in Word and Sacrament, nothing else. Its very presence in the world is a manifestation of God's grace; it is a place, a communion, that welcomes the lost and the broken, the very persons who can do more than raise their cry of longing, only to be heard: "I have seen the affliction of my

---

4. Michael Weinrich makes just this point concerning the churches of the Reformation when he states that "the church's strength lies in the knowledge that it is, in principle, weak." "The Openness and Worldliness of the Church," 413.

5. Koopmans, *De Nederlandse Geloofbelijdinis*, 128.

6. That discipline is added as a third mark will be discussed below.

people in Egypt, and I have heard their cry because of their taskmasters; I know their sufferings . . ." (Exod 3:7).

THE ATTRIBUTES OF THE CHURCH

Because Christ chose to dwell with this poor community, it continues to exist in its very poverty. It exists because God chooses that it continues to exist. As an existent reality, it can be described. The confessors of the Belgic clearly stated that they stood in continuity with the church of the ancient creeds (art. 9). The creed of Nicaea confessed the church as "one, holy, catholic and apostolic." The Belgic reflects those attributes in its description of the church, although it does not do so explicitly in all instances.

The Church Is One

"We believe and confess one single catholic or universal church . . ." This claim appears to fly in the face of reality. There are a host of churches, or church communions, many of whom lay an exclusive claim to represent Christianity—or did so historically. The Eastern and Western churches divided fairly early on. The Western church divided further in the Reformation, the Reformation churches themselves having continued to divide.[7] And this leaves out of the equation the ancient and oriental churches. To what does this claim lay witness?

The Belgic, in its own context, is saying to the king—and so to the world—that its confessors are not about establishing an alternate church. They are claiming continuity with the church as it exists, and as it can only exist—as one. They solve the problem of the plurality of churches with the simple claim that there is only one church. (Of course, there was no problem to be solved! It is our problem.) They will identify that church with certain "marks."

Still, we might ask of the confession: Of what does that unity consist? What makes for the unity of the church? The confession does not offer a direct answer, but nonetheless offers some hints. The first might be in the claim that the church has always existed and will always exist because it has Christ as "eternal King who cannot be without subjects" (art. 27). The

---

7. Lukas Vischer notes that the propensity to divide appears most striking among Reformed communions. "Communion: Responding to God's Gift," 25–29.

clue lies hidden for us. There was, in the late Middle Ages, the doctrine of the "king's two bodies."[8] According to this doctrine, the king's first body is his physical corpus, with arms and legs and brains, etc. The second body is the "body politic." The king's realm is his body. It is united in him—and he is responsible for the well-being of his body. By that reading, the church is one as Christ's body, a scriptural image (1 Cor 12) not cited elsewhere in this confession. And Christ's body cannot be divided.

The confession offers a second hint when the catholicity of the church (see below) is held together in unity, "in heart and will, in one and the same Spirit, by the power of faith" (art. 27). It is unity in the Holy Spirit, that is, unity in God as God is present contemporaneously with believers. Moreover, it is in "faith." This is not the claim that unity is achieved because Christians believe the same things, in the sense that they sign on to particular doctrines, however important that may be. It is that believers share in acknowledgement of their poverty and submission and trust in what God is about in Jesus Christ. This is not a faith that achieves something—unity—but one that receives: God's turn toward creation, which includes themselves. Faith is directed outward, away from the self of the community, toward the One in whom they *are* one—Christ.

We get a third hint in a "more effective" unity as believers "separate themselves from those who do not belong to the church . . ." (art. 28). Hence, unity is connected with holiness (see below), holiness understood as being made separate for God's sake. This is unity in the face of forces that would destroy the church through repression or banishment. It is a union that cannot be effected by believers on their own, however, because "this holy church is preserved by God against the rage of the whole world" (art. 27).

The members of the church are, moreover, "members of one another in the same body" (art. 28). As persons, they exist in communion. Our identity is constituted by our communion with others, strangers who have become sisters and brothers in Christ. We *are* one in the community that is Christ's body. This community is established and maintained in the sacramental life of the church (see below).

The Church Is Catholic

By confessing the church as "catholic," the Belgic again claims that its confessors are part of the full body of the church. The old notion of catholicity

8. Taylor, *Secular Age*, 161.

is of an orthodoxy as that "which is believed everywhere and always by all men."[9] We testify thereby that we are part of the church that holds to a common set of teaching and that across all boundaries. As this confession has it, the catholicity of the church is both diachronic and synchronic. The church consists of all the generations who are now members of the "church triumphant" as well as those spread across the globe, thereby transcending national, ethnic, racial, generational, etc., boundaries. The church has existed "from the beginning of the world," and so we are in communion with all our forebears (including those who walked this earth before Christ's appearance). But more, the church "will last until the end," and so we are in communion with all those who are yet to be born. This "historical" catholicity liberates us from a "presentism" that views all truth through the lenses of our current conceptual categories. It means that we give full attention to those who have gone before, confident that the Holy Spirit has worked with and through our forebears. But it also means that we have an eschatological perspective, expecting God's truth to come to us not only from the past, but from the future as well.

If catholicity is historic, it is also expressed in the full variety of expressions of the faith that come to us in the present. The church is "not confined, bound, or limited to a certain place or certain people" (art. 27). No one cultural expression of the faith holds either a monopoly or a priority in what constitutes the church. The only measure is in the "marks" of the church, none of which are ethnically, nationally, or denominationally circumscribed. Positively, the catholicity of the church means a transcending of boundaries. "The church's charge is to proclaim God's salvation, so that the boundaries are broken through . . . the church may not function as a fearful border guard, but as one who brings good tidings."[10]

The Church Is Holy

The confession uses the adjective "holy" to describe the church: "this holy church" (art. 27) and "this holy assembly and congregation" (art. 28). In what does its holiness consist? One the one hand, one can consider the holiness of its members. The saints live sanctified lives. The church manifests this as it exercises discipline, one of the three "marks" of the church: ". . . it

9. Vincent of Lerins, as cited by Kung, *Church*, 298.

10. Berkouwer, *Church*, 162. We will return to the question of how we confess catholicity (and unity) in our contemporary context below.

practices discipline for correcting faults" (art. 29). The Reformed churches understood their task as giving attention to the lives of its members. Since all are members of the same body, the pain of one member affects the entire body (1 Cor 12:26). How one lives one's life affects all. Moreover, the church cares for those who have gone astray, as for those who endanger themselves as well as others. So the church "separates" as it takes cognizance of its own members' lives. For Reformed churches, this would take place in the institution of the office of elder, whose specific task is, together with other elders, the oversight of the community of faith.

But holiness is not limited to discipline. The church is "set apart" by Christ. That happens by means of the main marks of the church, the pure preaching of the gospel and pure administration of the sacraments (art. 29). (Discipline exists only in relation to the first two marks as it pays attention to proper preaching and sacramental practice.) Believers separate themselves "according to God's Word" (art. 28). That is, God calls believers together in the promise and liberation of the gospel. Moreover, believers are gathered into Christ's presence in the use of the sacraments (see below). Nor is preaching the communication of religious information. It is the proclamation of the great glad news of God's victory over sin, death, and evil. The gospel, the Word of God (Christ), governs the church. It gives the church a particular shape and contour. Discipline, then, does a number of things. It pays attention to the preached Word, or more accurately, to the preachers of the Word. Is what they say in continuity with the gospel as received in Scripture? Is their conduct such that the messenger does not bring the message into disrepute? Are those who gather around the meal tended in the struggles and temptations of their daily lives? More than that, we will ask: Is the church, as institution and communion, in conformity with the gospel? Does its presence in the world give shape to the gospel it proclaims? To the extent that the marks are present, the church is holy.

The Church Is Apostolic

The Belgic does not explicitly mention the notion of apostolicity. That does not mean, however, that the notion is absent in this confession. It is present primarily in the marks of the church (art. 29). Apostolicity can be described as the church lives "in the discipleship, in the school, under the normative authority, instruction and direction of the apostles, in agreement with them, because listening to them and accepting their message."[11] To be apostolic is to maintain the integrity of the church in continuity with the apostles. In the Reformed tradition, this meant faithfulness to the message of the apostles, that is, to Scripture.[12] This finds expression in the preaching of the Word. Is the proclamation of the church in conformity with the message of the apostles? And so, is the congregation brought into the presence of the Lord of the church? Do those who preside at the Lord's Table stand in continuity with the church of the apostles? The answer to both questions has to do with the discipline of the church. As the church properly gives shape to its life through its office-bearers and its assemblies, it can claim to be apostolic.

NO SALVATION OUTSIDE THE CHURCH?

Few stretches of this confession appear more incongruous to our age than the claim in article 28 that "there is no salvation apart from" the church (we have not yet discussed article 36!). Does this not give an institution the power to effect salvation, thereby elevating it above God? Moreover, since the church is governed by humans (whether in a hierarchy or by the democratic rule of a congregation), is it not subject to corruption? Indeed, the Reformation movement was about responding to the corruption in the church! Cannot God work apart from the church? In fact, has not even the Roman church said as much when in Vatican II it acknowledged Christians beyond the boundaries of the church?[13] Many sincere believers have been estranged from the church for a variety of reasons, including unchristian actions of the church itself.

So how can we make sense of the Belgic's claim? Can we join with the Beglic in confessing this claim? In its sixteenth-century context, the confession is at pains to state that its confessors are neither leaving the church nor claiming that the church is secondary, a matter of indifference. In so doing, the confession accepts the old ecclesiastical claim of *extra ecclesiam*

---

11. Barth, *Church Dogmatics* IV/1, 714.

12. Berkhof, "De apostoliciteit der kerk," 196. Berkhof makes this connection through Ireneaus and Tertullian.

13. See the documents of Vatican II, particularly the declaration on "The Church," III/15, and on "Ecumenism," III, in Abbott, *Documents of Vatican II*. The Roman church does not grant other communions the designation as church, thereby leaving believers who gather in those communions outside the church.

nulla salus ("outside the church there is no salvation"). The ancient claim, however, is rooted in the notion that the sacraments are necessary for salvation, and that admission to the sacraments takes place by means of those authorized by the church—the clergy. But as we shall see, the old notion of the sacraments was at issue for the Reformers, and the power of the clergy to "dispense grace" was at the heart of what the Reformers contested. The discovery of the power of the Word, indeed of the Scripture as the written Word of God, could incline persons to understand that God, in *God's* freedom, could effect salvation apart from the church. So what is being claimed, or as we have been maintaining throughout this work, what is witnessed here?

On the one hand, the sacraments *are* involved. Baptism and the Lord's Supper are not merely symbolic actions that call to memory God's actions in Christ. They are ordained by God (!) "to seal his promises in us, to pledge good will and grace toward us, and also to nourish and sustain our faith" (art. 33). Moreover, they are not "empty and hollow signs," but "visible signs and seals of something internal and visible *by means of which* God works in us through the power of the Holy Spirit" (art. 33, emphasis added). We saw that the church is the gathering of those believers who are "washed by [Christ's] blood." In baptism, God signifies that *just as* water washes away the dirt of the body when it is poured on us . . . *so too* the blood of Christ does the same thing internally . . ." (art. 34, emphasis added). And in the Supper, Christ instituted "visible" bread and wine to "testify to us that *just as truly* as we take and hold the sacrament in our hands and eat and drink it with our mouths . . . *so truly* we receive into our souls, for our spiritual life, the true body and true blood of Christ" (art. 35, emphasis added). It is in the church that we receive these gifts.[14]

The confession does not make the connection with the sacraments directly. It supports its claim that believers are obligated to belong to the church with the notion that believers are "members of each other in the same body." This mutual membership (see 1 Cor 12 and Rom 12) is in the "body of Christ," and believers are united in Christ by means of the Spirit through the sacraments. But it is not through the sacraments alone. The sacraments are, as stated above, seals of the "promise," and the promise comes from God's own self, through God's speech, or Word. And the Word is proclaimed in and through the church. Now, it can be argued that the

---

14. That the confession does not understand the sacraments as under the control of the church and its ministers is to be discussed below in our reflection on the sacraments.

"message" of the gospel finds its way into the world by means other than the church.[15] That is true enough. Still, the "message," the gospel, has been carried by the church. The Scripture itself has been maintained, translated, and passed on by means of the church, the Christian community.

This all may still sound like an apology for the church. If, however, we hear the claim as testimony of believers, then it is the believer herself who simply claims that she cannot enjoy the delight of salvation, of communion with God, the wonder of the forgiveness of sins, outside the church. She has heard the impossible news that she is justified by an action of God in the person of Jesus in no other place than in the communion of saints. Moreover, the faith is not possible for persons on their own; they are united as one in communion. And if that communion is in Christ, then given the witness of Scripture, and of the Christian community, that communion is with one another, and so we are "members of each other."

This is not to claim that God does not and cannot work outside the church. Nor that those who have been estranged have been abandoned by God—although much to the church's guilt, the actions of the church may make that appear to be the case with the estranged. It is only to testify that it is only when, finally, one is drawn to the festal meal, to the wedding feast of the Lamb, that one knows the full joy of human flourishing in God's presence.

On the other hand, it is the startling witness that God works in and through the messy human phenomenon we know as the church. It is an impoverished communion, recall. And God chooses to dwell with broken sinners. It is as we are welcomed in all our humanity, including that human pride that desires to live apart from God, and so in our own misery, that we enter the wonder and delight that we designate with the word "salvation." God has turned toward us in Christ, chosen us and justified us, and we find no other place to be than in the church. And hence we are "obliged to join and unite with it, keeping to the unity of the church . . ."

GOVERNANCE AS A MATTER OF CONFESSION

If the church is recognized by its "marks," or essential characteristics, as the pure preaching of the Word, the pure administration of the sacraments,

15. Think, for example, of independent missionary societies, or Bible societies, or even local prayer and Bible study groups organized independently of an institutional church.

and the practice of church discipline, then "in short, it governs itself according to the pure Word of God." As stated above, the church was at issue in the sixteenth century. This confession was written in part to validate the claim that its confessors belonged to the "true church." That would mean, however, that this church as governed "according to the pure Word of God" would be governed differently than the false church, or the church that the Reformers rejected. How, then, was the church to be governed? The confession offers three articles on governance.

It is noteworthy that while governance *is* included in the confession (more on that below), it does not offer a detailed outline of governance. It does not, in short, offer a church order, even in attenuated form. It is very modest in its claim; that is, it does not make a detailed order a matter of church confession, hence not essential to the church.[16] It will speak only about the offices of the church and of the local church council. It says nothing of greater assemblies of the church.

It begins with the offices of the church, and then primarily of the office of the minister or pastor. It is his task (and in the context of the age, it was always a "his") to "preach the Word of God and administer the sacraments." If the church is constituted by the preaching of the Word and the administration of the sacraments, then persons are needed who are about that task. They are necessary instruments.[17] God accommodates God's self to the human by means of human servants, offices. As an office-bearer the minister represents the Other, God in Christ through the Spirit, to the church.

Here the confession breaks with the Roman church. It is in the context of ministers that the confession rejects the notion of the presence of bishops as authoritative in the church. Ministers share the "same power and authority, no matter where they may be, since they are all servants of Jesus Christ, the only universal bishop, and the only head of the church" (art. 31). Strictly speaking, this phrase only rejects the primacy of a "universal bishop," or pope. But reflecting John Calvin's view, the ministers themselves carry out the functions essential to bishops.[18] Moreover, *in practice* bishops proved themselves to be illegitimate (see below).

16. Noordmans remarks that a primary characteristic of Reformed church order is its intention to regulate ecclesiastical matters as little as possible. "Beginselen van kerkorde," 172.

17. Calvin remarks that "neither the light and heat of the sun, nor food and drink, are so necessary to nourish and sustain the present life as the apostolic and pastoral office is necessary to preserve the church on earth." *Institutes*, IV.3.3.

18. Calvin did not reject the notionsof bishops as such. However, he saw the bishops'

But the offices of the church are not limited to ministers, those who preach the Word and who administer the sacraments. The confession adds elders and deacons, who together with the pastors "make up the council of the church." The governance of the congregation is by council, not by person. With this move, the Reformed rejected governance by persons, whether it be by bishop or the charismatic leader. The confession claims that governance by "God's Word" is in the assembly of the offices, of three offices together.[19] This would institute a new way of church governance.

The confession does not describe the offices in detail, but it goes on to describe the functions of the offices. By means of the council of pastors, elders, and deacons "true religion is preserved; true doctrine is able to take its course; and evil people are corrected spiritually and held in check, so that also the poor and all the afflicted may be helped and comforted according to their need" (art. 30). In preaching the Word of God, ministers serve the maintenance of true religion and promulgate "true doctrine." To the extent that elders are engaged in discipline, they are a check on the ministers. But elders also watch over the spiritual life of believers, there to "hold in check" evil doers. The Spirit works through the elders in council as they guide believers, and the community, in its life and work. Moreover, the community tends to the poor and the afflicted. This "impoverished communion" includes those who have little means of personal support, either material or spiritual. As members of Christ, believers are members of one another. And the instrument for care is that of the deacons.

The confession spends an entire article outlining its belief that the office-bearers of the church be properly chosen. One can detect a resistance to the then current practice of the appointment of clergy, either through the church hierarchy or by the powerful in government and society. The confessors believe that God's chosen way is by a "legitimate election of the church." Negatively, this contests the political maneuvering by persons to obtain power and authority in the church. Positively, this is to free the proclamation of the Word and the presence of the sacraments from powerful forces that would use (and so abuse) God's way in the interest of one party or another. The confession does not prescribe (or describe) what a

---

function as that of ministers of the Word. His argument against bishops was that they were not faithful to the tasks entrusted them. He did not, however, consider the pope a proper bishop. *Institutes*, IV.6.

19. It is clear that this claim has been contested. No one model of the order of the church has full claim on Scriptural authority. This is, however, the rudiment of a presbyterial-synodical church order.

"legitimate election" looks like. It is, however, to free the church from outside powers. It is the church, the "impoverished communion," who elects its leaders, not those in power "from above."

Still, the church is to have an "order" as something useful and good, (art. 32). Such an order, however, is, as we have seen, to be modest. It rejects "human innovations," elaborate sets of laws imposed from without, and accepts "only what is proper to maintain harmony and unity and to keep all in obedience to God." While this sounds modest, it remains very open to the judgment of the leaders of the church as to what is necessary to "maintain harmony and unity."

CONTEXT

To what extent is the church a matter of *confession*? The church is a sociological phenomenon. We observe churches; we can study them; we participate in them. The church need not be confessed, but rather its reality is to be acknowledged. Still, the Belgic begins its turn to the church with the words, "We believe and confess one single catholic or universal church." Believers ("we") *confess* the church: "I believe in the Holy Spirit, the holy catholic church."

The Belgic confesses the church because the church is an *act of God*, not of humans. Yes, the church is a "holy congregation or gathering," and it appears on a Sunday morning that churchgoers choose to come together, and hence the church can be said to be a human institution. As indeed it is. However, it is *gathered* by God. The confession witnesses that God is active in establishing the phenomenon of the church. This has several implications. First, the church is not a "voluntary institution" as we might describe it from a sociological perspective, particularly in the American context.[20] That is, it is not a society of persons gathered around common religious interests. It does not live by virtue of its own genius or energy, its own plans, goals, techniques, etc. It is unlike any other sociological institution. It is established and maintained by God by the work of the Holy Spirit.

Here the paradox of the church's *visibility* and *invisibility* becomes manifest. As an institution, the church can become corrupt. This happens, of course, quite visibly. The confession speaks of the "false church," one that is easy to "recognize" (art. 20). It can be recognized as it "assigns more

---

20. Nor is the church *only* a legitimating social institution, as Peter Bergen maintains in *The Sacred Canopy*, 33f.

authority to itself and its ordinances than to the Word of God." The Belgic considers this in the context of its struggle with the then church of Rome. In our own age, one might ask whether the church spends more energy on theories of management and strategies of marketing that in does in listening to Scripture, even as scriptural injunctions might run counter to the measures of success offered by the culture. The false church does not "administer the sacraments as Christ commanded in his Word." Do believers gather without celebrating the sacraments of baptism and the Supper in ways that conform to Scripture's story? In the face of the degeneration of the church, God maintains the church against the powers of the age, often in ways that escape visible perception.

And yet believers witness gatherings where the story is told, where Scripture is read and proclaimed. Believers testify to communities that pay attention to the life of its members, of its communion, as it gathers around the Lord's Table—hence discipline. The community hence witnesses to societies as it embodies the gospel as the proclamation of the story gathers a people who are in fact "members of each other." Believers testify to communities where the proclaimed Word propels the community into mission in the world without, where the sacraments not only nourish faith, but point the community toward God's kingdom that is both present and future. As the liturgy for the Lord's Supper of the Reformed Church in America has it, ". . . this supper is a pledge and a foretaste of the feast of love of which we shall partake when we enter the kingdom of God."[21] The community of faith is *visible*.

Secondly, witness to the community of faith counters the rampant individualism characteristic of American religious life. Protestantism has borne the accusation of engendering and promoting religious individualism. According to Charles Taylor, the "buffered self" has it roots in the Reformation notion that the individual could approach God apart from the ministrations of the church.[22] Without gainsaying a kernel of truth in that assertion, the Belgic maintains that the church is a community, a congregation, a people. And believers are obliged to be members, not simply out of duty or in obedience to divine command, but because we are "members of one another." Our salvation is in the acknowledgment that to be truly human is to be in communion with God and consequently with one another.

21. *Worship the Lord*, 11.
22. Taylor, *Secular Age*.

Third, not only by confessing the church as "holy and catholic" but also by acknowledging the apostolic nature of the church in the "preaching of the gospel," the community testifies to a people who live in obedience to its Lord and not to the prescriptions of the norms and customs of the culture of its age. That means for North Americans, for example, that it does not live by the logic of consumer capitalism. It does not accept divisions of class and race, of social standing and language, of separation along ethnic lines. It lives by the promise of the kingdom of God, where all are welcomed at the wedding feast of the Lamb. This is manifest most clearly at the Lord's Table, Holy Communion, the Eucharistic feast.[23] To the extent that this takes place, the community witnesses not to the genius of its own action, but to the God who, in Christ through the Spirit, has created a communion where the "dividing wall of hostility" between "Jew and Greek" has been broken down (Eph 2:14), and there is "neither Jew nor Greek, slave or free, male nor female" (Gal 3:25).

The nature of this new communion is witnessed in another confession, the Confession of Belhar.[24] The central paragraph of that confession focuses on reconciliation. It is from this reconciliation that the church becomes one and that it advocates justice. The term "reconciliation" can also be rendered as "atonement."[25] The church is founded at the cross, as God turned toward the human and suffered the bloody consequences of sin that we humans might live. (John Calvin remarked that the church is built on the forgiveness of sins.[26]) The church's unity, then, comes not from its own resolve to reconcile with one another, but is in Christ. This, in turn is witness to a world that lives by various versions of "apartheid." The principle of separation may not be racial (although in fact the racial divide persists in American culture), but is also economic and cultural. The confession testifies to the fact that God is active with a human community, a community made up of sinful and fragile human creatures.

It must also be said, however, that the church is not only a community that is counter to the culture. By establishing a *human* institution, God

23. That this is often not the case is the "impossible possibility" of the church's sin. We can only note that the church as a human institution only proleptically participates in the eschatological communion, the fact of which does not excuse the church from the task of becoming what it is in Christ—one.

24. In *Our Faith*.

25. The original term in Afrikaans is *versoening*, which means both "reconciliation" and "atonement."

26. Calvin, *Institutes*, IV.1.20.

engages human culture in all its earthiness, its materiality, indeed in the messiness that is human participation. The church uses cultural forms in its prayer and its praise. Even in its simplest gatherings in modest church buildings, it occupies a particular form or shape that is both affirming and critical of its host culture. We confess that God is active not in separating believers from the world, but in sanctifying not only themselves but their world.[27]

Moreover, this community is led by persons appointed by God bring the alien and wondrous Word of the gospel to the community, a Word that the community does not own or have at its disposal but must come from without. And those chosen to lead are those called by God by means of the church, to govern not by the prescriptions of cultural norms and strategies deemed effective by its context, but by Scriptural norms. So, for example, those who lead are not to be like those who "lord over others," but "whoever would be first among you must be slave of all" (Mark 10:44). Or to offer another example, those who govern would also follow the Pauline principles that there is no division of "slave nor free, male nor female" (Gal 3:28) in this community.

This community, then, is a radically open community. The only "entrance requirement" is faith. And faith is to be understood as the Belgic has it. It is not adherence to a set of doctrines, but an open presence before God. It is to come before God in one's poverty, justified and empowered in one's humanity by God's action in the Spirit. As such, the community witnesses to the ways of God in the world that is present in the reality of the church, even a church as broken as the church often is. The confession is testimony to the acts of *God*.

---

27. The confession will come back to this point more strongly in Article 36.

8

SACRAMENTS

ARTICLES 33–35

NOT SURPRISINGLY, GIVEN THE context of its origin, the Belgic devotes a good bit of space to the sacraments. The sacraments were at issue not only between the established church and the Reformers, but among the Reformers themselves. Witness, for example, the divergence of the Lutheran and the Reformed following the fateful meeting between Martin Luther and Ulrich Zwingli in 1529 at Marburg, where the two Reformers could not reconcile their differences over the Lord's Supper. As we shall note, the Belgic wades into the battle, albeit very carefully. It attempts to walk a line between Roman Catholic material realism, Lutheran Christological convictions, and the anti-sacramental position of the enthusiasts. Here the Belgic manifests its Reformed character, although it must be said that here too the confession is not unique. Indeed, it picks up strands of thought that had existed in the church for some time.[1]

This essay, however, probes the question of how contemporary Christians can confess, or witness to the truth that is being claimed in this old confession. Are the old debates concerning the nature of the presence of Christ in the Supper, for example, still current? Is the question of rebaptism still at issue? Indeed, why sacraments at all? This chapter will attempt to argue that the sacraments *themselves* are a witness, not only as they stand

---

1. Seeberg, *Lehrbuch der Dogmengeschichte*, vol. 3, 508–12, offers a discussion of the debate between Thomists and Franciscans in which the options open to the Reformers were already present.

as an indication of something that took place "once upon a time"—the historical presence of Jesus of Nazareth—but of God's active involvement in history, a history that is not simply the past, but includes the present and the future as well.

As this chapter is being written, the United States has been captured by the issue of the presence of the Confederate flag flying over the capital of South Carolina. Passions run deep on both sides of the issue. For one group, the flag represents the advocacy of the right to hold slaves; it is a painful reminder of the terrible reality of racism, a virulent evil still manifest in the American culture. Another group claims that the flag represents an honorable past of those who gave their lives for the sake of a lost cause—state's rights. My point is not to take sides, although I think the first group is closer to the truth; rather it is that the flag as a symbol is more than a piece of cloth. It represents something profound. But it is more than representational. It is not merely a sign that points to another reality (rather like a road sign that shows me the way to Chicago). The flag, as symbol, is *part* of what it symbolizes. My point is that our ordinary lives are filled with symbols that capture us in a particular "world."[2] What the church calls "sacraments" are not completely strange, even to our secularized society.

SACRAMENTS AS ORDAINED BY GOD

Anyone who has spent time with a church at worship will have observed both baptism and the Lord's Supper, and may indeed have participated in them. They are ritual acts that by their practice manifest themselves as central to the church's worshipping life. So, at a superficial level, we know what they are, we can describe what we have seen, and perhaps even what we experience in their execution. They are evidently important, and have been for a very long time in the church. But what are they about?

The Belgic begins its discussion by stating that "we believe that our good God, mindful of our crudeness and weakness, has ordained sacraments for us . . ." (art. 33). The sacraments are "ordained" by "our good God." It is *this* God, the God we have confessed in the earlier articles, the God who turned toward God's beloved creation, who now turns toward us "weak" and "crude" creatures, not only in the gathering of the church, but in certain actions taken within the church, what we call "sacraments."

2. For an extended argument of how our lives are shaped by "secular liturgies," see Smith, *Desiring the Kingdom*.

This has two implications of import. First, the sacraments are not of our invention. They are not like other liturgical actions that may be useful in expressing our worshipful presence before God. *We* did not decide to have sacraments. We did not decide that they might be important, even crucial, for our lives. They come *to* us, and they come to us as an action of God, thereby manifesting God's gracious turn toward the human.

Second, the sacraments are not optional. They are not something that we could do without, should we choose to do so. There is a polemical edge to the confession in its original context; this is said against those who devalue the sacraments. But it also may need to be claimed in a church culture that would claim that the "real" matter is what happens through the spoken Word as God works on human hearts directly, "spiritually." From this perspective the sacraments (or "ordinances"), if practiced at all, are at best a sort of helpful reminder of the real matter, God's address to the human heart. But that cannot be the case, if the sacraments are ordained by God!

Why would God set these ritual actions aside for human use? The Belgic offers three reasons. First, it is a seal on God's promises. God not only turns to the world in speech, but that speech is *promise*. God beckons us forward. Promise is a fragile thing; it is given in the face of an unknown future. Who knows what circumstances might stand in the way of the fulfillment of promise? A couple promises lifetime love in a wedding. Circumstances may rise (violence of one partner against another, for example) that make keeping the promise at least problematic if not impossible. God's promises face the terrible reality of human sin evident in history's horrors. We are indeed "weak" and "crude." But is it human weakness when we consider that the promise of forgiveness is the promise of the impossible? This is all the more difficult given the sheer extent of God's promise. The Heidelberg Catechism (A 66) limits God's promise to "grant us forgiveness of sins and eternal life by grace because of Christ's one sacrifice accomplished on the cross." That's no small promise. But it falls far short of summarizing or including all of God's promises that come to us from Scripture. Perhaps the most prevalent promise in Scripture is God's promise that "I will be with you." And the promise of the kingdom or realm of God appears to be far from being fulfilled. In fact, a good deal of the biblical story gives evidence of God's people wrestling with the promise in the face of evidence that the promise remains unfulfilled.[3]

---

3. Perhaps the story of Abraham is paradigmatic in this instance. Through the Abrahamic cycle, the promise is endangered. And the fundamental promise given at

The sacraments place a "seal" on the promises, authenticating them, as it were, for us humans as we are ever and again prepared to give up on the promise. They *make* the promises real, real as in this-earthly reality, the reality that is our daily existence. Indeed, we perceive *God* working through them. Their "truth," what connects them with ultimate reality, is not ourselves, not our perceptions, not our reflection on them, but "Jesus Christ." God has turned toward us—as we have seen in earlier articles—and turns toward us still, through the Spirit. This *happens* in the sacraments.

Second, the sacraments are *themselves* promises, or "pledges." By God's action, they point us to God's good intention for us and for God's world. In this, as in the previous paragraphs, we meet the *eschatological* horizon of what happens in the sacraments. It has been remarked that the Belgic's reflections on the Lord's Supper, for example, lack this eschatological dimension.[4] But one notices that dimension here. In the sacraments we are pointed *forward*, toward God's future. Again, this is crucial for believers, faced as we are with a present that threatens to foreshorten the future.

Third, the sacraments are to "nourish and sustain our faith." In baptism and the supper, our fragile trust is sustained as we are drawn into intimate, physical connection with what God is about. It is not only what God *was* about in an historical past, although it includes that, but what God is about at *this very moment*. We are drawn into God's presence, not only in Word, as address, but in the depth of our humanity, what we designate by physicality as well as spirituality.

Hence, the confession goes on to say, there is something that goes on "externally" as well as "internally." This confession will use a sort of parallelism that is expressed by saying, with both sacraments, that "just as" something happens externally, "so also" something is happening internally. The confession is careful not to connect these two causally, as though what happens outwardly causes the internal to happen. The Reformers were careful to avoid any notion that the sacrament, *in its execution*, makes something happen. God's actions cannot be captive to human execution. Put crassly, the church could not dispose of or dispense grace through its sacramental acts. But at the same time, because these sacraments were ordained by God, they were not "empty and hollow signs" but "visible signs and seals of something internal and invisible, by means of which God works in us

---

the outset, that "by you all the nations of the earth shall bless themselves" (Gen 12:3), remains outstanding.

4. E.g., Koopmans, *De Nederlandse Geloofbelijdenis*, 169

through the power of the Holy Spirit." So there *is* a connection, but the connection is established by God's action "in us." We cannot perceive that action, but we can perceive the signs. They are trustworthy phenomena of God's action.

Reformed churches consider two rituals as sacraments within the framework of this confession: baptism and the Lord's Supper. This is a very restrained understanding of the sacraments; sacraments are not religious rituals where we sense God's presence—then they would be something *we* establish. We can only say that they are "ordained" by God because we have received them from God's Son, Jesus Christ. It was Christ who commanded his followers to "baptize" (Matt 28:20) and to "Do this in remembrance of me" (1 Cor 11:24).

BAPTISM: INCORPORATION INTO A NEW REALITY

The confession has testified to the appearance of Christ, this good God's only Son, whose atoning work on the cross effected forgiveness of sins (art. 21); that this same Christ is our righteousness, our "right relation" with God in all the world (art. 22); that indeed our blessedness, our justification, is in that forgiveness of sin (art. 23); and that true faith "regenerates us and makes us new creatures" (art. 24). As individual persons, we are incorporated into that reality as we are united with the church, the gathering of those "awaiting their entire salvation in Jesus Christ, being washed by his blood, and sanctified and sealed by the Holy Spirit." (art. 27). We are incorporated in the sacrament of baptism, for "by [baptism] we are received into God's church . . ."

Thereby the baptized enter the new reality established by God's turn toward creation at the cross and in Christ's continuing presence in the Holy Spirit. As a believer, "I am not my own, but belong—body and soul, in life and in death—to my faithful Savior, Jesus Christ."[5] The confession offers an image that at first glance looks familiar. The law has been fulfilled in Jesus Christ (art. 25) as his bloody death replaced the sacrifice of animals to atone for the sins of a people. Hence Christ "has put an end to every other shedding of blood, which anyone might do or wish to do in order to atone or satisfy for sins." The confession has already explored this dynamic, and this way of speaking is common enough in Protestant circles. A second look, however, allows the image to startle us with its relevance. We do not,

5. Heidelberg Catechism, A 1.

of course, sacrifice animals in our churches! What might it mean, however, that this is in fact the "end to every other shedding of blood"—even blood offered to atone? We shed blood all the time in war. We commend soldiers who give their "last full measure" for the sake of—well, for the sake of what? We sacrifice for the sake of peace and prosperity, freedom and justice. This to "atone." We execute criminals. Economic "progress" often enough ends in death. Take for example, former Communist lands, where countless individuals were sacrificed on the altar of the good of the whole. But before we Westerners discredit such examples as the behavior of an evil empire, it would be good to consider how in the West we set factories that dangerously pollute in neighborhoods where the poorest live, thereby sacrificing the weak at the altar of the economic health of the majority. What might it mean that Jesus' death is the end of the need to find scapegoats to sacrifice, to atone, a neverending cycle of violence?[6] We would have, then, the inbreaking of the kingdom of God, announced and initiated by Jesus. And the baptized enter that new, changed, reality.

A second image, also "bloody," and also familiar at least to Reformed thinkers, is that of circumcision. Baptism replaces the old covenant's ritual of circumcision as the sign of inclusion in the people of God. The image shifts, of course. The cross is not directly in view. Rather, incorporation into the people of God is. Again, however, this portrays the baptized as entering a new people, the people of God, the new Israel looking ahead, yes, to a fulfillment, but in another sense already a part of what God is about.

Both images, then, are not only about that which has happened. The cross has happened, of course. The believer enters that place where she is received, accepted, and so belongs in Christ because of what Christ has done. And yet this remains promise. We still live in a world of violence and bloodshed. The baptized now belongs to Christ, and so to Christ's people, "set apart from all other people and alien religions." This is to live in a world shot through with threat, with death, with "alien" powers vying for our allegiance and promising a "blessed" future if we but acknowledge them and pay (with cash as well as our bodies) them homage. At the same time, it is to live in the security that is not our own, but is in the good God who turns to us. This sacrament witnesses that "God, being our gracious Father, will

---

6. So René Girard's theological project: that Christ's sacrifice breaks the chain of violence and counterviolence. See among others his *Things Hidden Since the Foundation of the World.*

be our God forever." And it renews "our hearts and [fills] them with all comfort; giving us true assurance of his fatherly goodness."

But baptism is more than a ritual of initiation into the company of those who commit themselves to "Christianity." Something happens with baptism. Reformed folk are often heard to say what baptism is *not*. We do not believe, they claim, in "baptismal regeneration." We do not believe that the sacrament itself regenerates the believer. And indeed the Belgic claims just that: we are not cleansed "by the physical water." The church cannot direct the Spirit; it has no power to administer who does and does not receive the gift that is in baptism. However, the rejection of baptismal regeneration can also imply that the sacrament does little more than signify something that has *already* taken place: God's action at the cross and in the resurrection.

In fact, the dynamic described in the first paragraph of this section— forgiveness, purification, etc.—takes hold, as it were, in the sacrament of baptism. What happens externally, the washing that water effects, is a certain sign and seal of something that happens internally. The Spirit of God is at work. That is, God is present, actively present, in the sacrament, so that the "blood of Christ . . . washes and cleanses [the soul] from its sins and transforms us from being the children of wrath into the children of God." We are then prepared to live in this new reality, a history driven by something other than bloodshed. We become the people that God has intended us to be from the outset. We can live as a *people* (circumcision) that are "set apart" as a sign of the kingdom. We live then as a people of hope, by promise.

The confession draws two implications from its claim that in this sacrament Christ's blood initiates us into a new reality. Both implications were polemical in the immediate context of the confession, both directed against the Anabaptists.[7] Both, however, testify to a particular understanding of baptism. The first rejects the practice of rebaptism. Christ has brought about the end of bloodshed once and for all. His atoning death has already taken place. Moreover—and this is the point of the confession—once the believer has been incorporated into the new reality, this need no more be repeated than does a person's birth. To claim otherwise is to deny what God

---

7. And so, indirectly, appealing to the king. In the letter to Philip II, the appeal was made to "demonstrate our innocence concerning the crimes with which we are charged." Or, in effect: "We are not of the dangerous group that advocates insurrection against ruling authority!"

is about in *what God had ordained* (art. 33). The baptized can enjoy the comfort offered because they *are* part of this new people.

The second implication affirms the practice of infant baptism. This practice continues to be controversial, even among Reformed circles (most famously contested by none other than Karl Barth). It is not my intention to enter this discussion by totting up arguments pro and con. It is rather to point out the logic offered by the confession itself (and to ask below how the church can *confess* this practice in the present). If baptism incorporates the believer into a new reality, and that new reality takes provisional shape in the church as a sign of the kingdom, and if that happens as one becomes part of a people (as happened in circumcision), then all who are part of that community stand in that new reality. That would include children. And if Jesus' death was for them as well as for adults—"Christ has shed his blood no less for the washing of little children of believers than he did for adults"—then they should be baptized. The kingdom is not only for those who are sufficiently mature to make an informed choice. Such an assertion would fly in the face of the entire logic of the confession—that all is grace. "Let the little children come to me" (Mark 10:14), Jesus said against those who would erect barriers against those not mature enough to "understand" what the kingdom is about.

BAPTISM AS WITNESS

To confess is to *witness* God at work, we have said. What does it mean, then, to confess baptism? It is to point to God's work in gathering humans into a new reality, transforming them in the midst of the ritual activity of the church (!). We can say that this witness takes place in two ways. First is the witness of history. While we of course have no access to the interior lives of others, we see countless persons across both time and geography, of every nation and tongue, who are gathered into the community of faith. Moreover, we witness those whose lives have been liberated from servitude to the gods of the age. In earlier times, it was claimed that the "blood of the martyrs is the seed of the church" (Tertullian). The truth in that claim is that some confessed with their lives that they would not bow to a god other than the one manifest in Jesus Christ, the liberator of the lowly and the hope of the lost. Nor are the martyrs a thing of the past. We can point to more recent history, the confessing church in Germany in the 1930s, to take one example.

If the first instance of witness comes from history, a second is contemporary. Baptism takes place in churches every week. Persons are set aside, washed clean, and become part of the cadre that is a "sign of the kingdom." Ordinary churches give witness to those whose lives are set aside for the sake of the kingdom. Nor are these extraordinary "saints." They are neighbors and coworkers, engaged in education and government and business and child-raising. We witness that we are confirmed in God's promises that the Spirit has been at work as the ritual takes place. It is not that the ritual *itself* automatically (magically?) compels the Spirit to work, but that the gracious presence of the Spirit fulfills *God's* promise to be present in our midst. This is, for Christians, God's manifest presence as *this good God* turns toward humanity, lowly, individual human beings, and unites them with himself in Christ.

THE LORD'S SUPPER:
SUSTENANCE IN THE NEW REALITY

We have seen that the Belgic was written as an apology to the ruling power, claiming that the Reformers were not heretics, but confessed the faith of the church catholic. In their confession of baptism, these Reformers distanced themselves from the Anabaptists. De Brés and his compatriots held to baptism as practiced in the great church. The article on baptism, then, had a polemical edge. If baptism was at issue internally among those who were being separated from Rome, the sacrament of the Supper was much more controversial. The Belgic weaves its way between those who held this sacrament to be no more than a sign, an occasion to remember our Lord's death and resurrection,[8] on the one hand, and Roman Catholics on the other, who had imported (fairly recently in dogmatic history) the notion of "transubstantiation," by which the elements change their "substance," becoming the physical body and blood of Christ (even while their "accidents" remained as bread and wine). And the confession also distances itself from the Lutherans when it claims that "Jesus Christ remains always seated at the right hand of God the Father in heaven . . . ," thereby denying the notion of Christ's ubiquity, or omnipresence—which, given that it is Christ, divine and human, would be Christ's bodily presence. And yet, the confession is almost shocking in its realism that "we do not go wrong when we say that what is eaten is Christ's own natural body and what is drunk

8. Many of these were ironically called "sacramentarians"!

is his own blood." In this the confession does not stray far from Calvin's understanding of what goes on in the sacrament. He calls it a "spiritual mystery" that is "symbolized by visible signs, as our infirmity requires, but in such a way that it is not a bare figure, but joined to its reality and substance. It is therefore with good reason that the bread is called body, since not only does it represent it to us, but presents it to us."[9]

Thus described, the confession has a polemical, or negative, edge. It clearly wishes to testify to Christ's presence in the sacrament. To what end? The Supper was instituted by Christ himself, the confession claims, "to nourish and sustain those who are already regenerated and engrafted into his family, which is his church." The believer has been incorporated into a new reality, brought into the church, a sign of the kingdom. That new reality exists, however, within the context of a world where other gods compete for loyalty. Indeed, the human, inclined to listen to "other voices," including the "voice" of his or her own desires, will be strongly drawn away from life in this new reality. In fact, if the believer is to live *in* this world yet not be *of* it—and indeed, in this world *for the sake of* this world—then she will constantly live amidst the claims of those who seek to control this world. How can, for example, a church under oppression continue to hope when all signs of hope disappear and God seems to have "left the building"? If faith is coming before God with empty hands, what is to assure us that such is all we are left with, that nihilism has the final word?

Christ comes to be "with us." Indeed, that was Christ's promise: "I am with you always, to the end of the age" (Matt 28:20). And more, we are united with Christ in this meal. Just so, the confession uses the image of "two lives": "those who are born again have two lives in them. The one is physical and temporal . . . the other is spiritual and heavenly." At first hearing, this sounds like the description of a sort of split, or schizophrenic, way of being human: we have one foot in the physical and another foot in the eternal. Indeed, this could easily lend itself to an unbiblical understanding of the human creature: that our bodily selves are somehow lower and less real than our spiritual selves, that we spend time in the physical world, but our true home is non-physical or unbodily.

To take that route, however, would be to diverge from the main impulse of the Reformation. The doctrines of justification and election affirmed the value, before God, of this-worldly reality in which humans live and work. The Reformed, in particular, were not separatists or enthusiasts

9. Calvin, "Short Treatise on the Holy Supper," 147.

who looked away from this world. They had a lively sense that this world was not *all*, and that God's history transcended this earthly life. But God did not *devalue* this earthly life. In fact, in contradistinction from a more Roman Catholic approach, this life was not of a lower order, to be elevated by grace. Rather, the human, *as human*, was drawn into communion with God.

But if the image of two lives is not to be misunderstood, what gain does it offer? It acknowledges the ambiguous position of the human as she or he lives out his life within a world, a world that God wants to claim for Godself. The image simply claims that while we need food and drink to sustain ourselves in our physical existence, so in the new reality, where we have been washed clean and "born again," we also need sustenance, lest we fall prey to the allurements, the "glittering prizes"[10] on offer in our world, and so lose our humanity—which is, after all, what has been given back to us in baptism.

And what sustains us is not a what but a who. Indeed, we are sustained as we are brought into the "communion of the body of Christ." One the one hand, of course, that body can be considered the church; the church is Christ's body. But on the other hand, in this context the body of Christ is Christ's physical body, or better said, it is Christ himself, who is and remains both human and divine, and so embodied. The "truth" of the sacrament is, as we heard, "Jesus Christ" (art. 33). We become united with Christ as we receive into our souls the "true body and blood of Christ." It is Christ—not the specter of Christ, not the memory of Christ, not a "spiritual connection" with Christ, but Christ—who is and remains fully divine and human. So Calvin says, "it is necessary also to partake of his true humanity."[11] We are drawn into communion with Christ. Our identity is determined by this communion. And as we are united in this ritual, that is, as *God* works through the Spirit, we are sustained in our fragile and oft-wavering trust.

We noted in our discussion of the Trinitarian nature of God that we experience God's Trinitarian action in the Supper. God turns to us as *Christ communicates* himself to us. That is, Christ gives of Christ's self. In the Supper, we come with open hands and mouths, to receive and to be fed. These physical gestures may be seen as only symbolic—as though something can be "only" symbolic! And yet, so goes the witness, as we receive the Supper, God's Spirit is at work, and so Christ is as really present as I am sitting in

10. In reference to the old BBC series *These Glittering Prizes*.

11. Ibid., 146.

the pew or kneeling at the altar rail. This is a sort of Calvinist realism. As the Heidelberg Catechism has it, although Christ is in heaven and we are on earth, "we are flesh of his flesh and bone of his bone."[12]

If Christ remains in heaven, then there is a sense of Christ's absence as well as Christ's presence in the sacrament. So we have a paradox: Christ is both present and absent. Christ is with us and beyond us at the same time. Here the eschatological finds its way into the confession of the Supper, albeit that it reflects more of the spatial imaginary of its age than it does the temporal. The importance, however, should not be lost. We stand in both Christ's present and future, in Christ as he is "with us," and with Christ as he goes before us into the promised kingdom. For that reason we stand already, if but for a moment, if proleptically, in God's future realm, now present.[13]

This new reality has as its sign or *gestalt*[14] of the kingdom, the community of faith. Hence, the sacrament is to be celebrated *in communion*. Communion with Christ is communion with Christ's own, with all who are called into the new reality, all who have been incorporated into this new reality. That implies, however, a community that lives under discipline. That is, it is a community that pays attention to its life as God's people. To come to the Table, to participate, means to pay attention that one does, indeed, live oriented to the new reality broken forth in Christ. It does not mean that the communicant is pure. We don't have to be pure or perfect to come to the Table, as some older pietistic practices had it. We come as "poor, desolate souls," often enough having given way to temptation. It does mean, however, that we are rightly oriented. Liturgically, the community engages in common and personal confession of sin, to hear the comforting and liberating gospel of forgiveness. The community is constituted in Christ, and so *as community*, and *as Christ's community*, is prepared to come to the banquet.[15]

---

12. A 76.

13. A. A. Van Ruler, in his final essay, "Ultra-gereformeerde en vrijzinnige," 122, states that the Supper is not a "means" of grace, but that we stand already in the kingdom of God.

14. *Gestalt* as the form, or configuration, of its subject.

15. In the standard liturgy of the Reformed Church in America, the congregation first "approaches" God as it rehearses the baptismal liturgy in confession, assurance, and law, and then as it "hears" God it is constituted by God's Word in Scripture and sermon. Only then, constituted as community, does it come to the Supper.

Nor, finally, is this an inward turning, an introversion of the church. God so loved the *world*. The church does not exist for its own sake. Believers are not isolated individuals seeking a fulfilling relation with God. In the Supper "we are moved to a fervent love of God and our neighbors." Transformed and sustained, we are drawn from our own introversion (our sin) and into our true humanity, which is cohumanity. Our true humanity is to love God and to love our neighbor. The Supper then thrusts us outward.

Indeed, such is the witness of the New Testament. Those who gathered in the first communities of faith were, often despite themselves, pointed outward into a world that did not welcome them. In fact, our Lord's puzzling words from his own "Last Supper," the meal that founded our own celebrations of the holy meal, find traction here. As Matthew has it, Jesus concluded his institution of the Supper with the words, "I tell you, I will never again drink of this fruit of the vine until that day when I drink it new with you in my Father's kingdom" (Matt 26:29). The Supper draws us into God's history as it tends toward God's future, what the Gospels call the "kingdom of God" or the "kingdom of heaven."

THE LORD'S SUPPER AS WITNESS

As with baptism, the Supper witnesses in two ways, historical and contemporary. From the outset Christians have testified that they do not and cannot sustain themselves in faith. They are sustained from without, as it were, by God's action in the Holy Spirit. And that happens most intensely, paradigmatically, and really at the Lord's Table (although not only there, of course). Throughout dogmatic history, theologians and church authorities have differed over precisely *what* takes place in the Supper, sometimes to the point of dividing the church. Popular piety, moreover, has proposed all sorts of views, including the notions that are outlandish and heretical to even the most irenic and ecumenical believers. But the *what* (and the *how*) aside, *that* something particular takes place in the Supper has been testified by generations. The witness of the Reformed, as reflected in confessions like the Belgic, avoids metaphysical speculation, and simply testifies that Christ is fully present, that believers are united with him at that deep place, as at that internal place where food turns to sustenance, so that Christ himself becomes the "bread" that sustains.

This did not only take place in the past. Christians testify that it takes place each day as the community of faith is gathered, not on its own strength, around the Lord's Table. Perhaps this is best illustrated in contemporary art. *Babette's Feast*, a film that centers on a meal prepared for a strict Danish Lutheran sect, is a commentary on the Supper. Viewers observe as the old members of the sect are transformed by the meal itself. Forgiveness emerges, and love, new life, and hope, and the community becomes renewed and life giving. There is no mention of a "mode of Christ's presence" in the film. But those gathered at the table are drawn into a new communion. Christians see in the film a testimony to what takes place as the Supper is celebrated, and the new reality dawns in their midst. This is not, of course, provable. There is no experiment that can be set up to verify the claim. It can only be pointed to. And Christians do, with profound gratitude, or "eucharist."

CONTEXT

I have noted in passing the contemporary context in which the sacraments offer a testimony of what God is about. I have yet to consider how we can confess the sacraments themselves. Strictly speaking, the Belgic does not confess the sacraments, but confesses that God has ordained the sacraments and that God has done so through Jesus Christ. Christ has "put an end to bloodshed" (baptism) and has "ordained and instituted the sacrament of the Holy Supper." We confess, then, something that God *has done*. It is testimony to historical events. These ritual actions, whatever significance they may have for us subjectively, were not human contrivances. We engage in them as a matter of obedience. For that reason their originating meaning is not constructed from human religious need (although they do, in fact, meet human need, as noted in the confession and commented on above).

If we follow the trajectory of that testimony, however, we can discern something of the message to our contemporary context; we confess to what God is about today. Our context, of course, is variegated. We live in a (post) secular society. That is, it is resolutely secular, the product of modernity. It is what is often called "postmodern," a term that I noted above to mean that contemporary Western society is not held together by an overarching regulative narrative. Postmodernity is secular in the sense that Charles Taylor has described: a disenchanted world inhabited by buffered selves. *At the same time* it is "post"-secular. Western society has become a society where religious commitment has taken hold in the midst of resolute secularity. This is due, in part, to immigration patterns whereby large religious groups live in the context of secular societies (one thinks of Islam in France, or of religious communities in the United States). Those same immigration patterns bring a resurgence of Christianity to the old strongholds of the Christian West that had become more and more secularized.

The testimony to the God who ordains the sacraments meets this complex context as it points to the *historical* nature of what God is about. To the secular, enlightened human for whom the world has become "flat," where everything revolves around the present, the confession testifies of a larger world. This is not simply the mystery or the sense of awe that one encounters that suggests that there is more to reality than meets the senses. For this is not "vertical." It points to a God who was active in the past, that the past is present, and in promise points to the future, a future that is also present. This is transcendence, but it is historical transcendence, albeit one that testifies that God escapes what we are able to sense, what Immanuel Kant called the "noumena."

As historical, the Christian confession differs from the religious understanding that focuses on the sheer presence of mystery. Old pagan religiosity also majored in mystery. Idolatry is shot through with mystery. What until recently was called "New Age" (which in fact is very ancient) is mysterious. Many contemporary alumni of the church who consider themselves spiritual (and rightly so) testify to a sense that there is a "more" that they are ready to attribute to the "divine." But testimony to the fact that God ordains the sacraments is of a God who engages the world *historically*. That means, first of all, that it is a confession of *this* particular God, the God who turns toward God's creation in love, the God who meets us in Christ, hence the liberator God, the God who freed the slaves and the God who promises liberation.

And it means, secondly, that this same God engages humanity—us!—in God's historical action. The faith community testifies that *God*, the God who is incarnate in Christ, and so "Emmanuel," this God is present with this community in the present. *This community*! That is, this impoverished community, this gathering of sinners who await the full presence of God, is the place where God chooses to dwell! And if God chooses to dwell in this humble place, then this earth, with its history, with its pain and hurt, is where God chooses to dwell.

The testimony, then, is that for this good God, creation is good. God institutes rituals that take humble bits of created reality and gives them significance. Water, bread, and wine, these elements represent creation, and enter—literally enter—human reality and become instruments of God's intentions.

Just so, God establishes a community of faith, a new kind of people. This happens not by a sort of divine slight of hand. It happened and happens in Christ, a historical figure communicated by God's Spirit. The confession is not an apology that proves this to have happened. It is testimony by those who gather that *this* is what we acknowledge taking place. We are a people who did not constitute ourselves, but are established. It is a *critical* community. It stands not simply in contrast to all other communities, established as they are by human contract, but is critical in the sense that it displays what God intends for all creation.

Its critical nature can be seen in its stance to what has been called "moral Therapeutic Deism."[16] This way of thinking, distilled by researchers from American youth culture, holds the following:

1. A God exists who created and orders the world and watches over human life on earth.

2. God wants people to be good, nice, and fair to each other, as taught in the Bible and by most world religions.

3. The central goal of life is to be happy and to feel good about oneself.

4. God does not need to be particularly involved in one's life except when God is needed to resolve a problem.

5. Good people go to heaven when they die.

The God to whom Christians testify has been passionately involved with the creation. While this God cares intensely for individual persons and their flourishing—what baptism is very much about—the goal in life is not about the self, but about giving the self away for the sake of God's greater intentions. The sacraments lead one to the cross, to the place of a righteousness, a rightness, not simply for self, but for the love of neighbor, where God is present with the communion of saints along the historical way.

16. Billings, *Union with Christ*, 22.

9

THE COMMUNITY OF FAITH
AND THE SECULAR STATE

ARTICLE 36

ARTICLE 36 OF OUR confession, "The Civil Government," constitutes the most notorious stretch of the document. The phrase in the original confession that the government's task "extends also to upholding the sacred ministry, with a view to removing and destroying all idolatry and false worship of the Antichrist; to promoting the kingdom of Jesus Christ," etc., sounds completely outdated in our era where the separation of church and state has become a fixed article of faith in Western democratic society, as fervently defended by the churches as it is by those who are repelled by the thought that the churches could dictate social policy for the commonwealth. So difficult did this article become among Reformed churches that the Reformed Churches of the Netherlands (a denomination consisting of churches that broke away from the "public" Reformed Church in that country), and subsequently the Christian Reformed Church in North America, replaced the offending phrase with one more compatible with a modern understanding of the relative roles of state and church. This article may pose insurmountable difficulties to one hoping to be able to unite one's voice with the church that confessed (and confesses) faith as it is articulated in this document.

It is important, then, to understand that the confession is a product of its age, as much in its discussion of civil governance as it is in matters more usually considered by a confession. Hence it is helpful to recall the historical context of the confession at the outset. The nascent Protestant movement was under pressure from the rule of Philip II of Spain, the pious emperor who saw as his vocation the elimination of the Protestant heresy in his lands. Guido de Brès protested that not only were the Protestants not heretics (see the Introduction above), but they were also not rebellious subjects:

> Besides these hidden testimonies of our consciences, those who hold office and pass sentence and judgment in legal proceedings would be good witnesses that they never observed anything in us that leaned towards disobedience, nor did they discover in us the resolve in any way to militate against your Majesty, nor did they find anything that would disturb the common peace. Rather, they found that in our communal assemblies we pray for the kings and princes of the earth and in particular for you, O most gracious Lord, and for those whom you have authorized in the regime and ruling offices of the regions and countries of your domain. For we have been taught not only by God's Word but also through the constant instruction of our preachers that the kings, princes, and authorities are appointed by the ordinance of God. Besides, we have been taught that he that resists the magistrates resists the ordinance of God and will receive damnation. We acknowledge and maintain that by the eternal wisdom of God the kings rule and the princes determine justice.
>
> Briefly stated, we believe that they have their office not through injustice or despotism, but by God's own appointment.[1]

This was not special pleading. As we shall see, this reflects a Calvinistic understanding of the relation between the church and governing authority. Thus, we will examine Calvin's approach to the matter.

Still, while the historical background helps us to understand the confession, the question remains: Can we join our voices to this confession in the twenty-first century? Hence the issue before us is not simply whether the relation of church and government as expressed in the confession has any relevance to the current state of affairs. Rather, we have been about asking the question of *confessing*. That is, does this confession witness to how *God* is at work in the world, the world of twenty-first-century pluralist societies as well as that of a world just emerging from the Middle Ages, a

---

1. Kemps, "Guido De Brès' Letter."

world where kings (and queens) and princes ruled or aristocracies were emerging. We shall return to these questions.

A CALVINIST APPROACH

De Brès began from a theocratic perspective. That is, that governing authorities exist; indeed they are set in place by the grace of God and consequently are answerable to God.[2] John Calvin would put it that God has "lovingly . . . provided in this respect for mankind, that greater zeal for piety may flourish in us to attest our gratefulness."[3] God's providential care included the establishment of human government. Calvin was firm in his rejection of anarchy, on the one hand,[4] and those who advocated the absolute privileges of the princes, on the other.[5] He would claim that

> . . . civil government has as its appointed end, so long as we live among men, to cherish and protect the outward worship of God, to defend sound doctrine of piety and the position of the church, to adjust our life to the society of men, to form our social behavior to civil righteousness, to reconcile us to one another, and to promote general peace and tranquility.[6]

The government, then, has a twofold task: the promotion of the worship of God (the first table of the law), and the maintenance of mutual human life in society (the second table of the law). To those who would argue that with Christ's appearance governments have become superfluous, Calvin noted that we are not yet in God's kingdom. Indeed, we remain as sinners. Instead we are pilgrims on the way:

But if it is God's will that we live as pilgrims upon the earth while we aspire to the true fatherland, and if the pilgrimage requires such helps, those who take them from the human deprive him of his true humanity.[7]

It seems odd to twenty-first-century sensibilities that the government's task includes the "first table" of the law, that is, the honoring of God alone.

---

2. Verboom, *Kostbaar belijdenis,* 277.

3. Calvin, *Institutes,* IV.20.1.

4. Perhaps with the Anabaptists in mind.

5. Perhaps with Machiavelli in mind.

6. Calvin, *Institutes,* IV.20.2.

7. Ibid.

Calvin, however, saw it as a commonplace, shared by Christian believers and non-believers alike:

> If Scripture did not teach that it extends to both Tables of the Law, we could learn this from secular writers: for no one has discussed the office of magistrate, the making of laws, and public welfare, without beginning at religions and divine worship. And thus all have confessed that no government can be happily established unless piety is the first concern. . .[8]

The welfare of a society is rooted in its religion, the forsaking of which would be ruinous for a nation. We shall return to discuss the extent to which this may apply in the present polity of the nations.

Perhaps more understandable to contemporary sensibility is the government's responsibility to the "second table" of the law, that is, to maintain human society. Calvin cites the many Old Testament passages on the duty of the king for the welfare of the people (see, for example, Psalms 72 and 82). Magistrates, he says are "ordained as protectors and vindicators of public innocence, modesty, decency, and tranquility, and that their sole endeavor should be to provide for the common safety and peace of all."[9] Verboom comments, "The sword must ultimately function as servant to care for the welfare of the people and for the weak and vulnerable among them."[10]

To execute the task of governance, God establishes an "office of magistrate." This office parallels ecclesiastical office even if it is not to be confused with it. The magistrates have a "mandate from God." God does not put them in place merely on account of human "perversity." That is, governance is not only a sort of emergency measure necessitated by human sinfulness. Rather, governance was set in place by "divine providence and holy ordinance."[11]

Moreover, God grants to the government the "sword," the power of coercion, for the sake of humanity. Without that power chaos would reign. While magistrates are not to give in to base passions when yielding the sword—either domestically in executing justice or internationally in pursuing war—they are required to use it to promote peace:

8. Ibid., IV.20.9.

9. Ibid..

10. Verboom, *Kostbaar belijdenis*, 278.

11. Ibid., IV.20.4.

> But since they cannot perform this [duty to the second table] un-
> less they defend good men from the wrongs of the wicked, and give
> aid and protection to the oppressed, they have also been armed
> with power with which severely to coerce the open malefactors
> and criminals by whose wickedness the public peace is troubled
> or disturbed.[12]

In return, citizens owe obedience toward those who govern. There is, of
course, a limit; obedience to the human must not become disobedience to
God.[13] Nonetheless,

> . . . with hearts inclined to reverence their rulers, the subjects
> should provide their obedience toward them, whether by obeying
> their proclamations, or by paying taxes, or by undertaking public
> offices and burdens which pertain to the common defense, or by
> executing any other commands of theirs.[14]

This includes obedience to unjust magistrates. A wicked ruler is, says
Calvin, a judgment of God (See Zech 11:4–17).[15] God continues to care
providentially for the children of this world. While Calvin offers a cautious
opening to revolution against bad government, it is only under certain
conditions, and is in no way to be undertaken by individuals, but rather by
lower governing authorities.[16]

Finally, I conclude this rather long excursus by noting that Calvin is
clear that there are two realms of governance, the spiritual and the civil,
and they are not to be mixed or confused. The government is not to involve
itself in the work of the church, nor is the church to subsume the government under its power. That is not to say that the church has nothing to
say to those who govern. After all, those who govern have an "office" from
God. And how are they to know what God intends? That happens only
with knowledge derived from the sole authority on such matters, Scripture.
Hence, the church's responsibility is to speak *to* governing authorities.

---

12. Ibid., IV.20.9.

13. Ibid., IV.20.32. Calvin cites Acts 5:29 here.

14. Ibid., IV.20.23.

15. Ibid., IV.20.25.

16. Ibid., IV.20.31.

GOD'S GOVERNANCE

The Belgic reflects Calvin's understanding of the matter. On the negative side, the confession rejects the Anabaptist notion that the kingdom of God is breaking in and human government is not only unnecessary but can be viewed as part and parcel of sinful reality. In that context, the confession was written against the fear of anarchy occasioned by excesses of enthusiasm in the Anabaptist camp. In the Netherlands in 1535, for instance, when convinced that the Second Coming was happening, an Anabaptist was overcome by the Spirit and, convinced that the wearing of clothing was against the divine will (the original parents were naked in Eden), persuaded the assembled gathering to remove their clothes, throw them into a fire, and they began to run naked through the streets.[17] More notorious was the establishment of a communal experience in Münster, Germany, a polity built as the kingdom of God on earth, an experiment that ended in violence and chaos. As we saw above, the confession had a polemical goal of convincing the king that the Reformers distanced themselves from those who rejected all legitimate civil authority.

However, the confession takes this negative position because it argues, positively, that *God* has instituted civil authority, and the confession makes that argument on biblical grounds.[18] Still, this position coheres with the broad outlines of the confession itself. The good God who has disclosed God's self in Scripture has turned toward the world, the good creation. This is expressed in Article 13, on providence: "We believe that this good God, after creating all things, did not abandon them to chance or fortune, but leads and governs them according to his holy will, in such a way that nothing happens in this world without God's orderly arrangement." One could maintain that with the coming of Christ and the outpouring of the Spirit, this arrangement has reached a point where the "sword" of authority is no longer necessary. However, the confession's robust understanding of sin is such that this is not the case, "because of the depravity of the human race." Even the "saints" who construct utopian communities are not free from sinfulness, as the history of utopian communities has shown. Humans need to be protected from themselves. In God's graceful patience, God provides human government to maintain public peace and order.

---

17. Evenhuis, *Ook dat was Amsterdam I*, 42–43.
18. Citing, for instance, Rom 13:1; Prov 8:15; and Jer 21:12, among others.

Nor, one might argue, following Calvin's suggestions (above), is this simply a matter of law and order, providing a polity where humans do not degenerate to the rough justice of violence and counterviolence. This is for the protection of the weak and the vulnerable, for those whose interests are subject to those with political or economic power.

While the confession does not use the term, the "magistrates," those who govern, have an office no less than do those who lead and govern the church. With that *office*, they are responsible to God for how they exercise their function. This is the case whether or not they acknowledge their office, or even whether they acknowledge God. The confession is not, after all, a venture in political theory. As confession, it witnesses *God's* action in the world, and God has intentions for the created order, intentions scripturally codified in its story. Hence, it can be claimed that God cares particularly for the poor and the oppressed, for those who cry out in bondage. God's little ones are not to be used and abused. This is the case whether or not those in authority acknowledge the fact.

The responsibility for civil welfare does not fall to the church—or not directly so. This is the task of the government.[19] The church's responsibility is to remind the ruling authority of its God-given responsibility. The framework set out by the confession is often pictured as an ellipse with two foci, the church being one focus, responsible faithfully to bring the Word of God, with the government at the other focus. The church is not to replace the government, nor the government to direct the church. The church does, in the name of God, speak to ruling authority. Whether those who govern listen is another matter.

The confession goes a step further.[20] Not only does the government have the task of maintaining public order, but its task "extends also to upholding the sacred ministry," etc. As we saw above, this coincides with Calvin's view, which was a shared understanding of the time. In fact, Philip II saw just that as his sacred task as he attempted to rid his empire of the heretical Protestants! We can make sense of this if, on the one hand, we consider that public morality rests on shared religion. That is, the ethos of a society follows the contours of reality, and reality is rooted in who God is and what God is about. Or so the argument might go. On the other

19. This negates the notion that the care of the poor is the church's responsibility. The confession does not support "faith-based" organizations that are expected to replace the ruling authority in the care for the poor. This does not relieve the church of its diaconal responsibility, but it confesses that God uses ruling authority as a "ministry."

20. Or it does in the original text. We shall follow that text for the moment.

hand, we can make recourse to the fact that good governance is about the promotion of the humanity of the subjects of the polity. That includes, of course, restraint from murder, from theft, from all that threatens mutual trust. But true humanity also includes acknowledgement of the God who called the human into existence, as individual persons and as community. A Christian is compelled to witness that the God who called this human into existence is none other than the one who liberated the slaves from Egypt, and who gave up God's self at Golgotha for the sake of this broken and sinful human.

Indeed, this is for the "removing and destroying all idolatry . . . and promoting the kingdom of Jesus Christ." To the contemporary ear this sounds ridiculous, of course. Modern governments do not go after images[21] nor do they take sides for any one religion. Nonetheless, it is good to remember that despite their claim otherwise, a neutral state is an illusion—more, it is an impossibility. All government is built on certain values. We may agree on the values; we may even argue that the values are fundamentally Christian. But a value-free government is not possible. Tolerance, for example, is highly valued for the contemporary state. The state tolerates all points of view, including all religious points of view. A Christian, however, must acknowledge limits to toleration. The confession of Belhar, for example, is clear that a society cannot tolerate a doctrine of the separation of the races that result in apartheid. Moreover, Christians will advocate public policy positions that they derive from the values generated by the presence and demands of the kingdom of God. Moreover, they will see beneath the countervalues—racism, the sexualization of culture, the commodification of human relations, to take a few examples—the honor given to the gods or the idols of the age, those powers that promise salvation and deliver death. In this way, the church confesses that God has established those in authority to remove all false worship!

The altered text to the confession softens (and "modernizes") the claim that civil authorities are to uphold the sacred ministry by stating instead that they have the task of "removing every obstacle to the preaching of the gospel and to every aspect of divine worship." This is more congruent with the contemporary understanding of the separation of church and state. With the promotion of religious freedom, the "Word of God may have free

21.. As this is written, there is news that certain groups claiming to follow the dictates of Islam have destroyed antiquities, claiming to remove idolatry. Before Protestants get too heated over this, it is helpful to remember the iconoclastic outbursts at the outset of the Reformation.

course; the kingdom of Jesus Christ may make progress; and every anti-Christian power may be resisted."[22]

All of this leaves open the question of the plurality of religions, a reality of contemporary society, but something that could only faintly be envisioned, if it could be at all, in the middle of the sixteenth century. We shall return to this below when we consider the contemporary context of the confession.

CHRISTIAN CITIZENSHIP

If governing authority has an office from God, then the appropriate response of the populace is obedience. This, of course, has a limit, as the confession, like Calvin, refers to Acts 5:22, where we are to obey God rather than people, although the confession puts it negatively: we are to obey ruling authorities in "all things that are not in conflict with God's Word." It does, imply, however, that obedience is to those who rule who do not acknowledge the God of Israel, the Father of Jesus Christ.[23] This will include respecting those who have been appointed to govern as well as the payment of taxes! In so doing, even in the worst of times the believer acknowledges God's providential care for the creation.

Special mention should be made of the injunction to pray for governing authorities "that the Lord may be willing to lead them in all their ways and that we may live a peaceful and quiet life in all piety and decency." It is a particular form of support for governing authorities to intercede for them before God. Koopmans remarks that there is no more critical stance vis-à-vis governing authority than the church interceding for it.[24] As the church places the authorities before God, it expects God to guide the authorities in God's way, which on the one hand may sustain a current governmental policy, but on the other hand may well go against that policy or activity! Prayer is a confessional action in that it anticipates and expects *God's* action in the world for the sake of the world.

---

22. The phrase does not, of course, speak explicitly of "freedom of religion." That, however, is how such is exercised in the contemporary polity. However, it raises the question of coherence. If freedom of religion exists, then how is "every anti-Christian power" resisted?

23. So reflecting, e.g., Rom 13:2 or 1 Pet 2:13–14.

24. Koopmans, *De Nederlandse Geloofbelijdenis*, 198.

CONTEMPORARY EXPRESSIONS

Our review of article 36 has surfaced contemporary hesitations with the usefulness of this stretch of the confession for the church's confession today. We can note, however, a number of Reformed confessional documents that stand in the heritage of this article. They may assist us in reflecting on how—and whether—this confession can still articulate witness to what God is about. I will pass four documents in review, in the order of their historical appearance.

The first is the well-known Barmen Declaration.[25] Barmen did not claim a positive role for the government, but set out a clear separation from the ruling authorities. Its first point that "Jesus Christ, as he is attested for us in Holy Scripture, is the one Word of God which we have to hear and which we have to trust and obey in life and in death." Christians could follow no other leader (*Führer*). Moreover, there is no area of life that is not under Christ's rulership. Christ is "God's claim upon our whole life." Consequently, the declaration rejects "the false doctrine, as though there were areas of our life in which we would not belong to Jesus Christ, but to other lords." The declaration has as its audience the members of the evangelical churches in Germany (Protestants), and only indirectly the state. Nonetheless, it stands in the tradition that places the Word of God over and against ruling authorities.

More directly in the historical heritage of the Belgic stands *Foundations and Perspectives of Confession*, a 1950 confessional statement of the Netherlands Reformed Church. The document deals with civil authorities in its sixteenth chapter. There it makes the following claims:

1. That God has ordained civil authorities that the world is preserved for God's kingdom

2. That in God's desire to transform the world into God's kingdom, God has given civil authorities the task of restraining disorder, protecting the oppressed and punishing the wicked.

3. Governments that derive their "purposes and standards" from their own impulses risk unfaithfulness to their divine calling. Hence governments cannot be neutral nor adopt world views of their own choosing.

4. Citizens are obliged to support the government.

25. This confession can be found in *Book of Confessions*, 309–12.

5. Civil authorities and the church both serve God, but in different ways. The church "preaches God's salvation" and the civil government "regulates eternal life with a view to this salvation."[26]

This paragraph is set within a document that confesses God as king and the trajectory of history toward the kingdom of God. One might note the year of its adoption, 1950. The Dutch church had just emerged from a war where civil authority went badly wrong, threatening the continued existence of the Dutch nation.

Our third expression comes from the Reformed Church in America's "Our Song of Hope." Itself not a confession; it was adopted by the General Synod for "teaching" in the church. If *Foundations and Perspectives* turns around the kingdom of God, "Our Song of Hope" gives major space to the work of the Spirit. Two of its paragraphs speak of the work of the Spirit with human governments:

> As citizens we acknowledge the spirit's work in human government
>> for the welfare of the people,
>> for justice among the poor,
>> for mercy towards the prisoner,
>> against inhuman oppression of humanity.
> We must obey God above all rulers,
>> waiting upon the Spirit,
>> filled with the patience of Christ.
> We pray for the fruits of the Spirit of Christ
>> who works for peace on earth,
>> commands us to love our enemies,
>> and calls for patience among the nations.
> We give thanks for God's work among governments,
>> seeking to resolve disputes by means other than war,
>> placing human kindness above national pride,
>> replacing the curse of war with international self-control.[27]

Here one clearly sees the positive theme of the Belgic at the fore. Explicitly lacking is mention of the government's task to remove idolatry, although in seeing the Spirit at work eliminating war or standing against oppression, there is an implicit acknowledgement of the defeat of idolatry.

Our final expression comes from the Belhar Confession. It is particularly in its fourth paragraph (on God's justice) that this confession gives

---

26. *Foundations and Perspectives*, 27–28.

27. "Our Song of Hope," 153.

expression to the church's prophetic task vis-à-vis the governing authorities. Clearly, the government cannot be neutral, for it is to conform to God's justice, a justice that sides with the poor and the oppressed. It is *God* at work effecting reconciliation (atonement), and thereby establishing *God's* justice, including justice within human society. For that reason "the church . . . must stand by people in any form of suffering and need which implies, among other things, that the church must witness against and strive against any form of injustice, so that justice may roll down like waters, and righteousness like an ever-flowing stream." Furthermore, the church "as the possession of God must stand where the Lord stands, namely against injustice and with the wronged; that in following Christ the church must witness against all the powerful and privileged who selfishly seek their own interests and thus control and harm others."[28]

None of the four expressions noted here directly mirror the Belgic's article on civil authority. They do, however, display the confession's deep testimony to God's action in the world, using human government as God's providential instrument may be approached. One approach may be more prophetic as it calls government to task, while another might seem to grant governing authorities more leeway, indeed to be more optimistic. We shall return to this below.

CONTEXT

The Belgic was written within the context of Christendom. That arrangement no longer holds. Even the United States, a country that never knew Christendom as it was established in Europe, but nonetheless was for many years a Protestant culture, can no longer claim to be a Christian nation, at least not in its official polity. Western societies are ruled by an officially secularized state, one that is legally bound to non-interference in religious life and to tolerance of all religious points of view. What must the church confess in that changed circumstance?

It is not my purpose to wade through the theological question of the relation of church and state, of faith and culture. That would be an immense undertaking, one that has engaged many minds over the centuries. Even the debate over article 36 has engaged many thinkers, even as an expression of ecclesial division within the Reformed body. My question has to do with *confession.* Can we say anything about what God is about in relation to civil

28. Belhar Confession, quoted from *Our Faith*, 148.

authority? One can ask only secondarily what the particular stance of the church should be vis-à-vis governing authority. The answer to that question only follows on the first question: What is God about?

To answer that question, I ask a prior question: Does God get involved in history, or does God leave history to itself? Is history as we experience it a field of struggle between forces, where to the victor—the strongest—goes the spoils? Are we left with a Manichaean world, where the outcome of the battle between good and evil remains undecided? The confession's answer is, as we have seen, no. God does not abandon things "to chance or fortune, but leads and governs them according to his holy will . . ." (art. 13). God engages with history and, in fact, moves history toward God's purposed end.

This is the biblical witness, a witness to *promise*. The promise is of a society of *shalom* and righteousness (justice). It is a *promise*, the promise of the "new heavens and the new earth." Isaiah articulates the promise of a new society where infant mortality is no longer a reality, a society where people live on their own land, not as tenant farmers for the powerful, a new society where old enemies, natural enemies, become friends (Isa 65:17–25). Nor is this a utopian dream. The Old Testament witness is that God sent "shepherds," rulers, to guide God's people into a society where people could live as true and free humans.

This is not, however, the realization of human ideals of peace and harmony. This is God's way to a future that not only escapes our imagining, but finds its way through human recalcitrance. It judges our ideals, ideals that can wreck terror. Van Ruler, commenting on Zechariah 13:7, notes that the way to God's future is not one of gradual, undisturbed progress toward our dreamt-of future. God intervenes by "striking down" even the good ruler, the "good shepherd." The way forward is through crisis.[29] The Good Shepherd himself was crucified. God's way with the world is through the cross. Nonetheless, even as the world appears to come apart, God has not abandoned the world to its own fate, but remains engaged. This is the "good God" of the confession. The upshot is a firm confidence in God's guiding hand.

I illustrate this with witness not from Christian sources, but from a Jewish one. In the face of a terror that cannot be explained or systematized (to do so would be to deny the reality of evil), the Holocaust poet Micheal O'Siadhall writes in a poem entitled "To Life!":

> On the lookout, ready for any fate

29. Ruler, *Heb moed voor de wereld*, 133.

Dabrowa Tarnowska's prayer-shawled
Rabbi Isaac would wait
With followers. Found and hauled
From their hide-out underground,
They're herded to a Jewish graveyard.
Someone unseen by their guard
Passes a vodka bottle around
And facing each waiting assassin
They drink their toast *lachayim!*
As linking hands they begin
To dance. At once mowed
Down. A preventable episode.
Enraged the squad cuts
Their bellies and tramples on them
To spill their mutinous guts.
Praise him with timbrel and dance.[30]

Chaos and evil reigned. The governing authorities clearly act against God's promise. And yet the people dance. This enrages authority. But authority exists only as responsible to God, whether or not authority acknowledges the fact. A people remains—very few in number, perhaps—as witness

Writing from the context of a secularized society and in a country whose government is officially "neutral," Wim Verboom acknowledges that the confession does not directly apply to the current context. Still he persists with the confession by putting the matter in the form of a dream. He *dreams* of a government within which "streams of the future Lordship of Christ already begin to appear. Streams where weak and vulnerable humans are sustained and those on the margins of society are cared for." Verboom's dream includes civil authority that both avoids and battles against contemporary forms of idolatry by appropriate means. As idols he mentions the materialization, "economization," bureaucratization, and sexualization of society as wells as the "cruel idols" of discrimination and nationalization, particularly anti-Semitism.[31] Verboom offers an eschatological confession: this is what God is about and believers dare to hope in this future. This is not theocracy that degenerates into dystopia, for it emerges not from human idealism, but from the good God who intends only good for God's creation.

---

30. In O'Siadhall, *Gossamer Wall*, 83 (emphasis in original).
31. Verboom, *Kostbaar belijdenis*, 291.

The church has been witness to history for more than two millennia. In that that time, it has known rulers and governments that have fostered human flourishing and rulers that have been oppressive. Most often, the rule has been a mixture. We do not live in God's promised future. Moreover, the church has witnessed surprising turns in history. We cannot be too hasty in evaluation of the turn of events, claiming that behind them we see God's good hand. That would lead the way to ideology. However, the church witnesses that in the midst of chaos, in the darkness, we believe, we trust, that God is at work. This is a difficult but tenacious faith, perhaps allowed only to a few.

Still, we live in the context of a religiously pluralist world. Those of other religions are no longer separated by national borders, let alone continents. Our neighbors and coworkers are often not Christian believers. They are not secularists either, but followers of another faith. Can we confess that God has established governing bodies to promote Christianity? We can, it seems to me, advocate Christian values as God-given, and expect the government to promote them. But we surely cannot claim that God sets up government actively to promote Christian worship. We can, however, claim that God establishes rulers to promote the flourishing of human persons, and that includes not only respect for religion, but provision for religious exercise. This is the good God who turns toward creation and humanity.

10

LAST JUDGMENT

ARTICLE 37

THE FINAL ARTICLE OF the Belgic would appear to present a particular obstacle to discovering in this confession a contemporary testimony to the
faith. I have maintained that confession is *witness* to what God is about.
But how can we witness to what has not yet taken place? We can, of course,
look to Scripture, as indeed this confession does, and as countless attempts to catch a glimpse into God's future have done over the centuries.
Nonetheless, that approach tends to use Scripture as a repository of gnomic
passages that rightly discerned plot out, and paint, the end of history as
we know it. Instead, I will suggest that this confession in fact occasions a
way in which contemporary Christians can—and do—testify to a hope, a
"well-founded hope."[1]

A MODEST ESCHATOLOGY

First, however, a few remarks on article 37 itself as it concludes the entire
confession. In the first place, it is not simply an appendix to the previous
articles. It is not as though the main business has been completed and the
confessors had to add a piece about the "end" for the sake of completeness.
In fact, "end" has a double meaning. It can mean that things have come to
the place where nothing more happens. It is the "end of the line." It is the

1. Berkhof, *Well-Founded Hope*.

final stopping place. History ends; it goes no further. But "end" can also mean goal, that toward which a process or a history aims.

The "last judgment" is the end in both senses. In fact, the previous articles of the confession point in this direction. The original intentions of the good God find their fulfillment and completion in the "last things," the *eschaton*. "All of Christian teaching and Christian life must be understood as preparation for the last and the decisive. The resurrection and the second coming of Christ determine the complete existence of the Christian church on earth."[2] We have seen that as God turns toward God's creation, God involves God's self in *history*. The incarnation of the Son is God fully involved in history. But history is not history without an end, a *telos,* without that toward which it moves. Otherwise, it is caught up either in recurring cycles or is a chaotic play of forces. The notion of *judgment* means that there is a *meaning* toward which history tends. History is measured against its intended goal. It is *judged*.

In the second place, the Belgic presents a modest eschatology. In fact, any number of themes that are included in a theological eschatology are not present here. There is no mention, for example, of Israel. Nor does the confession say anything about heaven or hell. Nor does the confession choose among the various millennial options: pre-, post-, or a-millennialism. For that matter, there is no apocalyptic speculation here, nothing of what we have learned to know as dispensationalism.[3] Instead, the confession restricts itself to a scriptural report on the coming of Christ and his judgment. As Koopmans put it, the eschatology of this confession is presented as it is in the New Testament, and can subsequently be summarized in two words: Jesus comes.[4]

Jesus comes in the manner that he had ascended. That is, it is the *resurrected* Jesus, the Jesus who is both human and divine, who comes. This means that God has remained involved with humanity in the interim, in the time of our history. The unfolding of history as we know it, with its peaks and with its horrors, has not been abandoned by God. God has been present in God's Spirit. And God has paid attention, as it were, because the triune God remains intimately involved as God's own self in our flesh as the ascended Christ.

---

2. Koopmans, *De Nederlandse Geloofbelijdenis*, 203

3. Which would be anachronistic, of course! On dispensationalism, see Marsden, *Fundamentalism and American Culture.*

4. Koopmans, *De Nederlandse Geloofbelijdenis*, 205

JUDGMENT AND HISTORY

Christ comes to judge. This sounds ominous to contemporary ears rather like the bad old religion of guilt and punishment. This is judgment that consigns non-believers to eternal damnation; and since a good portion of the world falls into that category, this is not good news at all. However, the absence of judgment would be very bad news indeed! For then history is left to the rule of the most powerful. God would have withdrawn from the field of history and let things play out as they may.

As I noted above, judgment means that history is going somewhere. Put in biblical terms, it moves toward the kingdom of God. We are not there yet. We "are and remain God's people on the way. The Kingdom of God is not here and not there."[5] This fact alone is comfort. We are not trapped in the world as it is. Nor are we caught in a senseless play of forces.

More than that, in the last judgment, everything becomes transparent. So much of what happens in history is hidden behind appearance. Often enough that is intentional. Propaganda poses as truth. Abuse of power is dressed out as policy intended for the common good. The victims of abuse and violence are silenced and hidden. The truth disappears as history moves forward, and history's record is written by the victors. But if a time of judgment comes, then the hidden secrets of history are laid bare.

And they are judged. That is, as Van Ruler put it, "the earth must be swept clean of all unrighteousness and violence. Evil must be rooted out."[6] Evil cannot exist in God's kingdom, not in a kingdom of God's love. The good God we confess draws history to its close where "all shall be well." The vagaries and cruelties that dominate history will be no more. Not only individual persons, but the oppressed peoples of the earth can catch a glimpse of an end when all shall be made right. A "great reversal" takes place and the "oppressed are liberated and the oppressors are punished."[7] This is eschatology as liberation.

The transparency that engages history includes the individual person, which means that *my* own history is laid bare. I am judged. This is not a pleasant prospect, given that "all have sinned." In fact, the secrets that are manifest are likely secrets even to myself! I have buried my hypocrisies, my deceits, the little cruelties I have inflicted, my refusal to acknowledge

---

5. Verboom, *Kostbaar belijdenis*, 303.

6. *Ik geloof*, 7th ed. (Nijkerk: Callenbach, n.d.), 121.

7. Verboom, *Kostbaar belijdenis*, 315.

the pain of others, all from myself. Had I been aware of the truth about myself, I could not live with myself. The fact that God judges me means that God takes me seriously. I am responsible before God. God takes my history seriously. I do not disappear in the mass of humanity, hidden away from history in my little corner of the world.

THE JUDGE

All of this is unbearable. It certainly appeared that way when the confession was written. Popular piety was dominated by a fear of hell. And the last judgment was portrayed as grim indeed. One need only observe the tortured souls in Hieronymus Bosch's *The Last Judgment,* or those on Christ's left hand in Michelangelo's painting in the apse of the Sistine Chapel. Indeed, when we are made transparent to ourselves, our *own* judgment would be that of condemnation.

However, the Judge that is confessed in the Belgic, the Judge who appears in Scripture, is Jesus. The Judge is our Savior! "Our hope is in the Judge, who is our Savior, the Judge who despite our past has a future for us because He has broken the power of the past by His cross and resurrection."[8] The Judge is not a distant ruler; he is the one who not only shared our skin, who wrestled with temptation, who wept and struggled with us, but who was crucified on our behalf. The stunning upshot is that in him the last judgment has *already* fallen in history.[9] That is, the last judgment is not simply something that we await, but it has already taken place! Our individual sin has been judged and Christ has taken the resulting pain inside Christ's self. His death is the "full satisfaction" (art. 21) that sets us right. The atonement points us toward the last judgment. It makes the unbearable bearable. *He*, Christ, is our rightness before God.

Hence, the prospect of judgment will be horrible for the wicked—we might say, for those who cannot accept the judgment that has already taken place their behalf. But it is "great comfort" to the "righteous and the elect" because what has begun at the cross will be brought to fulfillment. I hasten to add that the "righteous and the elect" are not the self-righteous, but those who look away from themselves, who are drawn out of their own presumption. The elect are indeed the last and the least—the least of which is the guilty!

8. Koopmans, *De Nederlandse Geloofbelijdenis*, 209.
9. Van Ruler, *Ik geloof*, 122.

LIVING IN HOPE

The confession concludes as De Brès and his fellow believers look forward in hope. This look to the future has particular resonance in the context of its composition. As I noted above, it was an era in which individuals lived in fear of eternal punishment. A person could always wonder: Did I do enough? Was I pious enough? One thinks of Luther's anguish prior to the stunning insight that occasioned his actions that lit the fuse on the Reformation. But more immediately, the Reformers in the southern Netherlands (what is now Belgium) feared for their own lives under Philip II's campaign against the heretical "Protestants." And in fact De Brès would be among those who would die a martyr's death. The confession of hope "we look forward to that great day with longing . . ." was an existential testimony.

From whence that hope? The hope is in the Judge, the one who is, as we have noted, Savior and Judge. The Judge is the one who died on the cross, there to bear the sentence that would rightfully be brought against humanity—and individual humans. This insight leads us back into the central stretch of the confession. This Messiah is the one whom God sent to rescue humanity from itself. He is the one whose atonement justifies the sinner as God accepts the Son's self-offering on behalf of the sinner. The sinner's rightness is alien to himself or herself, but is in Christ, so that the Judge recognizes this rightness in the sinner. Moreover, the sinner has become right in action as the Spirit sanctifies her.

While it has rightly been remarked that the Belgic's take on the last judgment predominantly focuses on individual persons—the righteous and the unrighteous are judged—it does not neglect the larger picture. The one who comes "will burn this old world, in fire and flame, in order to cleanse it." The good God who turned toward creation rescues not only the lost human, but the creation itself. God engaged, and engages, history, the history of humanity, and the history of the creation. Final judgment is not simply about the separation of good and evil in relation to persons, but that the *world* is cleansed. This *is* judgment of the world. The world cannot continue as it is, where evil does its work, where death and destruction, oppression and ruin, destroy God's "beautiful book." Judgment does not, however, mean the elimination of creation. Judgment comes to purify, to make the creation what God intends. Believers confess that God has already begun to do just that. In fact, God has *done* that decisively in Jesus Christ.

The hope engendered in Christ grants to these believers, believers who face death—and that includes them all—a place, a "citizenship in heaven."

Peter addresses his readers as "exiles" scattered across Asia Minor. The Father has given "us a new birth into a living hope through the resurrection of Jesus Christ [the Judge!] from the dead and into an inheritance that is imperishable, undefiled, and unfading, kept in haven for you . . ." (1 Pet 1:3, 4). As Koopmans put it, ". . . the true center of our existence, the fatherland of our heart, is elsewhere."[10] This is true for the individual, of course. But it is also true of a *people*. The Reformers were not simply individuals; they were a community. We can say more. To the extent that the church is not simply the collection of souls fortunate enough to have heard the gospel, but are, like Israel, the firstfruit (Jas 1:18) of the coming of the nations (Isaiah's great vision), then this hope, this "fatherland," is the destiny of the nations of the earth. The promise that set the biblical story in motion in Genesis 12, that all the nations of the earth would bless themselves in Abraham, awaits. The community of faith is *already* conscious that the center of its existence rests elsewhere, and that elsewhere is not simply "above," in transcendent spatial realms, but "ahead," awaiting us in the future. We acknowledge that reality in the sacrament of the Supper when we say that that meal is "a pledge and foretaste of the feast of love of which we shall partake when his kingdom has fully come, and with unveiled face we shall behold him, made like unto him in his glory."[11]

CONTEXT

Two very different conceptual worlds form the religious context in which we might confess the last judgment. The one emerges from theological reflection in the past half-century or so, a sort of rediscovery of eschatology. This is highlighted by the theology of Jürgen Moltmann, introduced by his *Theology of Hope*, and as a major theme in the theology of Wolfhart Pannenberg.[12] Theologians began to consider eschatology as more than a sort of epilogue to history, as God's final act, so to speak. Instead, the end affects, or may even determine, history. God draws or beckons history forward. Creation looks toward completion. What God is up to in Christ is directed

---

10. Koopmans, *De Nederlandse Geloofbelijdenis*, 210.

11. *Worship the Lord*, 11.

12. Although it had been present much earlier in biblical studies and in theological circles in the Netherlands, particularly in the theology of Van Ruler. Velema characterized Van Ruler's theology as "thinking from the end." Velema, *Confrontatie met Van Ruler*.

toward the end. Someone like K. H. Miskotte could talk about the "surplus" of Scripture, meaning that God's promises as we hear them in the Old Testament have not all been fulfilled, but remain outstanding.[13] The swords have not been beaten into plowshares, nor spears into pruning hooks (Isa 2:5); tanks haven't become school buses or bullets melted into plumbing for housing for the homeless. We might confess the last judgment in this context, admitting that the Belgic does not operate in the same conceptual world as late-twentieth- and early-twenty-first-century theology.

In a very different religious conceptual world, we live amidst those with what might be called a more fervent apocalyptic approach. This approach is manifest in the immensely popular *Left Behind* series of novels, or in Hal Lindsey's *The Late Great Planet Earth*. This approach probes biblical apocalyptic literature for clues that map out the historical end of life on earth. It speaks of the "rapture" of believers, of millennial peace, of the identity of the "beast" in Revelation, and the like. Very often, it reflects the dispensational theology of the early twentieth century, by which history and its end is divided into various "dispensations." For many, this way of talking and thinking is what is meant by eschatology. In this context, the approach of the Belgic Confession is very modest indeed. It restricts itself to the coming of Jesus Christ as judge. It refuses to speculate on whether Christ will return before or after the millennium of peace. We are not committed by this confession to engage an apocalyptic conversation. In fact, the Belgic can hardly be called apocalyptic, although it shares with apocalyptic literature the theme of hope and the overcoming of the forces of evil.

Still, most believers do not live within the conceptual world of academic theology, nor in a context where the nature of the "rapture" forms conversations that are of existential concern. Nonetheless, while the term "last judgment" sounds hopelessly old fashioned, we do live in a context that asks: Can we hope? And *what* can we hope? At the end of the Cold War, Frances Fukuyama wrote of *The End of History and the Last Man*. It was a book without hope. If history ended with the fall of Communism and we are left with the status quo, then there is nothing more than a world where the strongest survive and the weak are destroyed. There is nothing to hope for, nothing more than the interplay of forces. We are left to violence against violence, recrimination for past injustices, as the formerly oppressed become the new oppressors. Scientific evidence confronts us with

13. Miskotte, *When the Gods Are Silent*, 173–302.

the change in climate that threatens life on Earth as we know it. Are we condemned to the extinction of life—largely due to human action?

In any case, the question remains: If everything ends is death, then what does it *mean*? What does it mean to live in communities? What does it mean to struggle to overcome the terrible and terrifying realities of racism, or poverty, of illness? Is there any purpose to it all? The confession maintains that history is not over, that we are still pilgrims on the way, because we confess the particular God who moves us forward to an end where there is judgment. That is, to a time when good and evil are sorted out.

Three contemporary Reformed statements of faith articulate hope in a time bereft of hope. The first is from the Reformed Church in America's "Our Song of Hope." It begins:

> We sing to our Lord a new song;
> We sing in our world a sure Hope:
>   Our God loves this world,
>   God called it into being,
>   God renews it through Jesus Christ,
>   God governs it by the Spirit
>   God is the world's true Hope.
> We are a people of hope
>   waiting for the return of our Lord.
> God has come to us
>   through the ancient people of Israel,
>   as the true Son of God, Jesus of Nazareth,
>   as the Holy Spirit at work in our world.
> Our Lord speaks to us now through the inspired Scriptures
>   Christ is with us day to day.

And the entire work concludes:

> God will renew the world through Jesus,
> Who will put all unrighteousness out,
>   purify the works of human hands,
>   and perfect their fellowship in divine love.
> Christ will wipe away every tear;
>   death shall be no more.
> There will be a new heaven and a new earth,
>   and all creation will be filled with God's glory.[14]

14. "Our Song of Hope," 151–55.

The piece sets all history against a future hope. This is hope confessed in our own difficult time.

The Christian Reformed Church in North American, another communion that accepts the Belgic Confession as part of its confessional foundation, adopted a "contemporary testimony" in 2008, titled "Our Word Belongs to God." That testimony concludes:

> Our hope for anew creation is not tied
> to what humans can do,
> for we believe that one day
> every challenge to God's rule
> will be crushed.
> His kingdom will fully come,
> and the Lord will rule.
> Come, Lord Jesus, come.[15]

The Belhar Confession does not use an eschatological grammar. Nonetheless, reconciliation is such that while it has been accomplished in Christ, has not yet been fully realized. The unity of the church is not only a "gift" but is also a "task," something that awaits. And God's "justice and true peace among people" remain a hope. The Belhar can only be confessed in hope in the God who has not only acted in Christ but remains active.

All three examples of Reformed confessional action testify to the sovereignty of the good God. God is not stymied by human recalcitrance and the final fulfillment of God's intentions remain a focus of hope, a hope to which believers testify in a world that places its hope in something else—in fundamental human goodness, in technological planning, in the power to do good, in the benevolent interplay of the invisible forces of market or nations or heroic struggles. The confession focuses on God, whose actions in history point us forward beyond history.

CONFESSING THE LAST JUDGMENT

We are left with the question that I put at the outset of this chapter: How are we to testify to, give witness to, that which has not yet taken place? To what do we point? We can, of course, testify to a hope that we have within us. But how do we account for that hope (1 Pet 3:15)? How is that hope something

---

15. In *Our Faith*, 175.

more than a subjective desire, albeit a desire that has been shared by count-less generations?

The response is, I think, given in the well-worn notion of "already and not yet." That is, that we can witness to what *has* taken place, and what does take place, seeing in the very essence of the object of our testimony a direction to the future. Put concretely, we have noted throughout our re-flections that we can testify to the person of the Messiah as well as testifying to the work of the Holy Spirit. God has acted in our midst. And in Christ and through the Spirit, God gives us to live confidently toward the future. Jesus Christ was, and is, about the kingdom after all, a kingdom the signs of which have happened in our midst, but point forward. Jesus Christ was crucified, but was raised and has gone before us in the ascension, with the promise that he will come "in the same way as you saw him go into heaven" (Acts 1:11). The Spirit was poured out onto the believers and the Spirit continues to work, the Spirit's work pointing forward. God remains active.

We give witness that we have heard God speak, God's Word in Scrip-ture (art. 3). Those Scriptures are filled with promise, promise for the future. The promise is for a broken world, that a creation that has been besmirched will be purified. God's promises have been "sealed" in the sacraments (art. 33). For the individual person, the promise is of resurrection and of a judg-ment that will make all things well. The promise is of a community and a communion where "the home of God is among mortals. He will dwell with them as their God; they will be his peoples, and God himself will be with them; he will wipe away every tear from their eyes. Death will be no more; mourning and crying and pain will be no more, for the first things have passed away" (Rev 21:3, 4). We can witness that the promise has been provisionally and really fulfilled in Christ. The Spirit wakens hope within us and within our community. On that basis we look forward with hope.

CODA

THIS ESSAY BEGAN WITH the question: To what extent can the church confess the Belgic Confession? Can it unite its voice with the church of the sixteenth century? In the various chapters, I wrestled with how that might be the case. Is this old confession more than a period piece, honored and acknowledged as formative of our faith, but set aside as a historical curiosity? As I hope is clear from what I have written, I have found that the Belgic sometimes surprises with occasions where we can unite our voices with it. Whether the reader concurs is a matter of her or his decision. However, because it is a confession of the *church*, the answer to that question involves more than personal decision or inclination. The matter of confession is a matter for the church.

As such, our journey through the confession poses a number of challenges to the church. At issue, primarily, are the apostolicity and the catholicity of the church. First, consider the apostolicity of the church. Apostolicity asks: Is the church that confesses the *same* church as the church of the apostles? Is it faithful to its origin? Or to put it another way, is it the church of Jesus Christ, and not a church that finds its source elsewhere and offers allegiance to other gods? In its claim to be orthodox, our confession from the sixteenth century is at pains to connect with the church of the earliest centuries, and indeed to the Jesus as witness in Scripture.

The language, the concepts, and the interests of the Belgic can seem distant from us. There are biblical themes that make fresh claims on the contemporary church that are not addressed, or are addressed only indirectly, in the Belgic. The biblical emphasis on the created order as God's good creation is of fundamental interest to the contemporary church as the world faces the crisis of climate change and its threat to life on earth. The focus on the salvation of the individual may seem overemphasized in a world where individualism has become a problem. Nonetheless, if the

Belgic was faithful to the church in its earliest configuration around Jesus, then its interests and its articulation challenge our own interests. Even as we confess anew in the language and context of our own age (consider, for example, the Belhar Confession and the Barmen Declaration), the Belgic challenges us to consider its own themes and even in the dress of its old language. If, for example, there is an overemphasis on individual salvation, and an under emphasis on the justice of God as a corporate expression of human community, perhaps we need to be reminded that the individual person is not lost from God's sight.

The challenge, however, does not rest there. We do not live in the sixteenth century. We live in a new context. Indeed, the text takes on new meanings in a new context, as I have endeavored to explore. *How* we articulate our understanding of the faith can take old language and translate it in a new vocabulary. In this way, the catholicity of the church is at issue. This is a catholicity that is communion with our forbears of the sixteenth century—and their descendants. Their vocabulary may be alien to us, but we remain in communion with them, and so listen with them not only to the witness of Scripture, but we listen to their own expression of the faith. Indeed, even if we put our confession in new words, our own vocabularies, with their attendance concepts, have histories. We live in communion with the past.

But the challenge is to articulate the faith in the present. That task demands a new vocabulary. Nonetheless, that means building a new vocabulary with an ear for what our communion has said and to what needs to be said today.

But what *must be said* today? Dirkie Smit, in answering the question, "What is *status confessionis*?," says that the church is in a "state of confession" when "a moment of truth has dawned when *the gospel is itself at stake*."[1] That is, the church is in danger of trading the gospel of Jesus Christ for the gods of the age. The church would then lose its center or core. It would no longer have a reason to exist. But the danger is not simply that an institution may disappear. Far worse, the church would have nothing to offer a world that is dying without the gospel. I hasten to add that God can, and one presumes would, take other measures for the sake of God's beloved creation. But the church's *raison d'etre* is to be the instrument chosen by God to proclaim the gospel in what it is and what it does. Confession is a way of articulating a witness to the gospel. *This*, it claims, is what must be said, and it must

---

1. Smit, "What Does *Status Confessionis* Mean?," 20 (emphasis in original).

be said here and now. Recall Barth's definition of confession, as noted in the Introduction, that a Reformed confession is formulated "by a Christian community within a geographically limited area, spontaneously and publicly, with provisional authority, and is a description of the provisional insight currently given to the universal Christian church into the revelation of God in Jesus Christ, as he is attested in Holy Scripture."[2]

So the challenge the Belgic puts to us is: How do we confess Christ today, in our own context? Does the Belgic itself offer content to that confession? We grant that the Belgic is not comprehensive in its explication of biblical themes. In fact, as we've noted, biblical themes that demand confession today are not present. So, for example, the Belhar Confession focuses on the themes of reconciliation, unity, and justice. And in fact, the Belgic itself was appended, as the great Synod of Dort filled out the Belgic's statements on election.

Moreover, it is clear that many of the Belgic's concerns are not our own. The social and political context in which article 36 was written, for example, is not our own, and we cannot simply adhere to the confession's claims. In addition, the Belgic was written against the background of the Roman church, with both its doctrinal claims and ecclesiastical institution—as well as against, particularly, the Anabaptists. Those traditions have shifted and developed, as has the Reformed tradition. The joint declaration on justification by the Lutherans and the Roman Catholics, for example, has profoundly shifted the relationship between Rome and the Reformation churches, on precisely that issue that effected the rent in Latin Christianity in the first place.[3]

Still, can we join our voices with the Belgic? Can we unite with it in confession of a particular God, the God who speaks to us in Scripture, who meets us in Jesus of Nazareth, the God who turned toward God's creation and acted in sheer love for the creature? This is a God who is active in history and beyond history in the creation and the eschaton. This is a God who gathers us into a communion of believers and who is present with us not only in Word and sacraments, but who is engaged in all of life. We will say it and sing it differently than our forbears did in the sixteenth century. But must we not sing it still?

2. Barth, *Theology and Church*, 112.

3. See "Joint Declaration on the Doctrine of Justification."

APPENDIX
THE BELGIC CONFESSION

THE VERSION PRINTED HERE is from the most recent translation completed jointly by the Christian Reformed Church of North America and the Reformed Church in America and published in *Our Faith*. Used here by permission.

ARTICLE 1: THE ONLY GOD

We all believe in our hearts
and confess with our mouths
that there is a single
and simple
spiritual being,
whom we call God—

    eternal
    incomprehensible,
    invisible,
    unchangeable,
    infinite,
    almighty;
    completely wise,
    just,
    and good,
    and the overflowing source
        of all good.

ARTICLE 2: THE MEANS BY WHICH WE KNOW GOD

We know God by two means:

First, by the creation, preservation, and government
of the universe,
since that universe is before our eyes
like a beautiful book
    in which all creatures,
    great and small,
    are as letters
    to make us ponder
    the invisible things of God:
        God's eternal power and divinity,
        as the apostle Paul says in Romans 1:20

All these things are enough to convict humans
and to leave them without excuse.

Second, God makes himself known to us more clearly
by his holy and divine Word,
as much as we need in this life,
    for God's glory
    and our salvation.

ARTICLE 3: THE WRITTEN WORD OF GOD

We confess that this Word of God
was not sent not delivered "by human will,"
but that "men and women moved by the Holy Spirit
spoke from God."
    as Peter says.[1]

Afterward our God—
    with special care
    for us and our salvation—
commanded his servants, the prophets and apostles,

1. 2 Pet 1:21.

to commit this revealed Word to writing.
God, with his own finger,
Wrote the two tables of the law.

Therefore we call such writings
holy and divine Scriptures.

ARTICLE 4: THE CANONICAL BOOKS

We include in the Holy Scripture the two volumes
of the Old and New Testaments.
They are canonical books
with which there can be no quarrel at all.

In the church of God the list is as follows:
In the Old Testament,
 the five books of Moses—
  Genesis, Exodus, Leviticus, Numbers, Deuteronomy;
 the books of Joshua, Judges, and Ruth;
 the two books of Samuel, and two of Kings;
 the two books of Chronicles, called Paralipomenon;
 the first book of Ezra; Nehemiah, Esther, Job;
 the Psalms of David;
 the three books of Solomon—
  Proverbs, Ecclesiastes, and the Song;
 the four major prophets—
  Isaiah, Jeremiah[2], Ezekiel, Daniel;
 and then the other twelve minor prophets—
  Hosea, Joel, Amos, Obadiah
  Jonah, Micah, Nahum, Habakkuk,
  Zephaniah, Haggai, Zechariah, Malachi.
In the New Testament,
 the four gospels—
  Matthew, Mark, Luke, and John;
 the Acts of the Apostles;
 the fourteen letters of Paul—

---

2. Jeremiah here includes the Book of Lamentations.

to the Romans;
the two letters to the Corinthians;
to the Galatians, Ephesians, Philippians, and Colossians;
the two letters to the Thessalonians;
the two letters to Timothy;
to Titus, Philemon, and to the Hebrews:
the seven letters of the other apostles—
one of James;
two of Peter;
three of John
one of Jude;
and the Revelation of the apostle John.

ARTICLE 5: THE AUTHORITY OF SCRIPTURE

We receive all these books
and these only
as holy and canonical,
for the regulating, founding, and establishing
of our faith.

And we believe
without a doubt
all things contained in them—
not so much because the church
receives ad approves them as such
but because the Holy Spirit
testifies in our hearts
that they are from God,
and also because they
prove themselves
to be from God.

For even the blind themselves are able to see
that the things predicted in them
do happen.

ARTICLE 6: THE DIFFERENCE BETWEEN CANONICAL AND APOCRYPHAL BOOKS

We distinguish between these holy books
and the apocryphal ones,
    which are the third and fourth books of Esdras;
    the books of Tobit, Judith, Wisdom, Jesus Sirach, Baruch;
    what was added to the Story of Ester;
    the Song of the Three Children in the Furnace;
    the Story of Susannah;
    the Story of Bel and the Dragon;
    the Prayer of Manasseh;
    and the two books of Maccabees.

The church may certainly read these books
and learn from them
as far as they agree with the canonical books.
But they do not have such power and virtue
that one could confirm
from their testimony
any point of faith or of the Christian religion.
Much less can they detract
from the authority
of the other holy books.

ARTICLE 7: THE SUFFICIENCY OF SCRIPTURE

We believe
that this Holy Scripture contains
the will of God completely
and that everything one must believe
to be saved
is sufficiently taught in it.

For since the entire manner of service
which God requires of us
is described in it at great length,

no one—
    not even an apostle
    or an angel from heaven,
    as Paul says—[3]
ought to teach other than
what the Holy Scriptures have taught us.

For since it is forbidden
to add to the Word of God,
or take anything away from it,[4]
it is plainly demonstrated
that the teaching is perfect
and complete in all respects.

Therefore we must not consider human writings—
    no matter how holy their authors may have been—
equal to the divine writings;
nor may we put custom,
nor the majority,
nor age,
nor the passage of time or persons,
nor councils, decrees, or official decisions
above the truth of God,
    for truth is above everything else.

For all human beings are liars by nature
and more vain than vanity itself.

Therefore we reject with all our hearts
everything that does not agree
with this infallible rule,
    as we are taught to do by the apostles
    when they say,
        "Test the spirits
        to see whether they are from God,"[5]

3. Gal 1:8.
4. Deut 12:32; Rev 22:18–19.
5. 1 John 4:1.

and also,
"Do not receive into the house
or welcome anyone
who comes to you
and does not bring this teaching."[6]

ARTICLE 8: THE TRINITY

In keeping with this truth and Word of God
we believe in one God,
who is one single essence,
in whom there are three persons,
really, truly, and eternally distinct
according to their incommunicable properties—
 namely,
  Father,
  Son,
  and Holy Spirit.
The Father
 is the cause,
 origin,
 and source of all things,
  visible, and invisible.

The Son
 is the Word,
 the Wisdom,
 and the image
  of the Father.

The Holy Spirit
 is the eternal power
 and might
  proceeding from the Father and the Son.

Nevertheless,
this distinction does not divide God into three,

6. 2 John 10.

since Scripture teaches us
that the Father, the Son, and the Holy Spirit
each has a distinct subsistence
distinguished by characteristics—
yet in such a way
that these three persons are
only one God.

It is evident then
that the Father is not the Son
and that the Son is not the Father,
and that likewise the Holy Spirit is
neither the Father nor the Son.

Nevertheless,
these persons,
thus distinct,
are neither divided
nor fused or mixed together.
    For the Father did not take on flesh
    nor did the Spirit,
    but only the Son.

    The Father was never
    without the Son,
    nor without the Holy Spirit,
    since all these are equal from eternity,
    in one and the same essence.

There is neither a first nor a last,
for all three are one
in truth and power,
in goodness and mercy.

ARTICLE 9: THE SCRIPTURAL WITNESS ON THE TRINITY

All these things we know

from the testimonies of Holy Scripture
as well as from the effects of the persons,
especially from those we feel within ourselves.

The testimonies of the Holy Scriptures,
which teach us to believe in this Holy Trinity,
are written in many places of the Old Testament,
which need not be enumerated
but only chosen with discretion.

> In the book of Genesis God says,
>> "Let us make humankind in our image,
>> according to our likeness."
> So "God created humankind in his image"—
>> indeed, "male and female he created them."[7]
>> "See, the man has become like one of us."[8]

It appears from this
that there is a plurality of persons
within the Deity,
> when God says,
> "let us make humankind in our image"—
and afterward God indicates the unity
> in saying,
> "God created."

It is true that God does not say here
how many persons there are—
but what is somewhat obscure to us
in the Old Testament
is very clear in the New.

For when our Lord was baptized in the Jordan,
the voice from the Father was heard saying,
> "This is my Son, the Beloved";[9]

7. Gen 1:26–27.
8. Gen 3:22.
9. Matt 3:17

the Son was seen in the water;
and the Holy Spirit appeared in the form of a dove.

So in the baptism of all believers
this form was prescribed by Christ:
    Baptize all people "in the name
    of the Father
    and of the Son
    and of the Holy Spirit."[10]

In the Gospel according to Luke
the angel Gabriel says to Mary,
the mother of our Lord:

    "The Holy Spirit will come upon you,
    and the power of the Most High will overshadow you:
    therefore the child to be born will be holy;
    he will be called Son of God."[11]

And in another place it says:
    "The grace of the Lord Jesus Christ,
    the love of God,
    and the communion of the Holy Spirit
    be with all of you."[12]

["There are three that testify in heaven,
the Father, the Word, and the Holy Spirit,
and these three are one."][13]

In all these passages we are fully taught
that there are three persons
in the one and only divine essence.
And although this doctrine surpasses human understanding,

    10. Matt 28:19

    11. Luke 1:35

    12 2 Cor 13:14

    13. 1 John 5:7—following the better Greek texts, the NRSV and other modern translations place this verse in a footnote.

we nevertheless believe it now,
    through the Word,
waiting to know and enjoy it fully
    in heaven.

Furthermore,
we must note the particular works and activities
of these three persons in relation to us.
    The Father is called our Creator,
        by reason of his power.
    The Son is our Savior and Redeemer,
        by his blood.
    The Holy Spirit is our Sanctifier
        by living in our hearts,

This doctrine of the holy Trinity
has always been maintained in the true church,
    from the time of the apostles until the present,
    against Jews, Muslims,
    and certain false Christians and heretics,
        such as Marcion, Mani,
        Praxeas, Sabellius, Paul of Samosata, Arius,
        and others like them,
        who were condemned by the holy fathers.

    And so, in this matter we willingly accept
    the three ecumenical creeds—
    the Apostles;, Nicene, and Athanasian—
    as well as what the ancient fathers decided
    in agreement with them.

ARTICLE 10: THE DEITY OF CHRIST

We believe that Jesus Christ,
according to his divine nature,
is the only Son of God—
    eternally begotten,
    not made or created,

for then he would be a creature.

He is one in essence with the Father;
coeternal;
the exact image of the person of the Father
and the "reflection of God's glory,"[14]
    being like the Father in all things.

Jesus Christ is the Son of God
not only from the time he assumed our nature
but from all eternity,
    as the following testimonies teach us
    when they are taken together.

    Moses says that God created the world;[15]
    and John says that all things were created through the Word,[16]
        which he calls God.
    The apostle says that God created the world through the Son.[17]
    He also says that God created all things through Jesus Christ.[18]

And so it must follow
that the one who is called God, the Word, the Son, and Jesus Christ
already existed before creating all things.
Therefore the prophet Micah says
that Christ's origin is "from ancient days."[19]
And the apostle says
that the Son has "neither beginning of days
    nor end of life."[20]

So then,
he is the true eternal God,

14. Col 1:15; Heb 1:3.
15. Gen 1:1.
16. John 1:3.
17. Heb 1:2.
18. Col 1:16.
19. Mic 5:2.
20. Heb 7:3.

the Almighty,
whom we invoke,
worship,
and serve.

ARTICLE11: THE DEITY OF THE HOLY SPIRIT

We believe and confess also
that the Holy Spirit proceeds eternally
from the Father and the Son—
    neither made,
    nor created,
    nor begotten,
    but only proceeding
    from the two of them.

In regard to order,
the Spirit is the third person of the Trinity—
    of one and the same essence,
    and majesty,
    and glory,
    with the Father and the Son,
being true and eternal God,
    as the Holy Scriptures teach us.

ARTICLE 12: THE CREATION OF ALL THINGS

We believe that the Father,
when it seemed good to him,
created heaven and earth and all other creatures
from nothing,
by the Word—
    that is to say,
    by the Son.

God has given all creatures
their being, form and appearance
and their various functions

for serving their Creator.

Even now
God also sustains and governs them all,
according to his eternal providence
and by his infinite powers,
  that they may serve humanity,
  in order that humanity may serve God.

God has also created the angels good,
that they might be messengers of God
and serve the elect.

  Some of them have fallen
    from the excellence in which God created them
    into eternal perdition;
  and the others have persisted and remained
    in their original state,
    by the grace of God.
  The devils an evil spirits are so corrupt
  that they are enemies of God
  and of everything good.
  They lie in wait for the church
  and every member of it
  like thieves,
    with all their power,
  to destroy and spoil everything
    by their deceptions.

  So then,
  by their own wickedness
  they are condemned to everlasting damnation,
    daily awaiting their torments.

For that reason
we detest the error of the Sadducees,
  who deny that there are spirits and angels,
and also the error of the Manicheans,

who say that the devils originated by themselves,
    being evil by nature,
        without having been corrupted.

ARTICLE 13: THE DOCTRINE OF GOD'S PROVIDENCE

We believe that this good God,
    after creating all things,
did not abandon them to chance or fortune
but leads and governs them
    according to his holy will,
in such a way that nothing happens in this world
without God's orderly arrangement.

Yet God is not the author of,
and cannot be charged with,
the sin that occurs.
For God's power and goodness
are so great and incomprehensible
that God arranges and does his works very well and justly
even when the devils and the wicked act unjustly

We do not wish to inquire
    with undue curiosity
into what God does that surpasses human understanding
    and is beyond our ability to comprehend.
But in all humility and reverence
we adore the just judgments of God,
which are hidden from us,
    being content to be Christ's disciples,
      so as to learn only what God shows us in the Word,
        without going beyond those limits.

This doctrine gives us unspeakable comfort
since it teaches us
that nothing can happen to us by chance
but only by the arrangement of our gracious
heavenly Father,

who watches over us with fatherly care,
sustaining all creatures under his lordship,
so that not one of the hairs on our heads
(for they are numbered)
nor even a little bird
can fall to the ground
without the will of our Father.[21]

In this thought we rest,
knowing that God holds in check
the devils and all our enemies,
  who cannot hurt us
  without divine permission and will.

For that reason we reject
the damnable error of the Epicureans,
  who say that God does not get involved in anything
  and leaves everything to chance.

ARTICLE 14: THE CREATION AND FALL OF HUMANITY

We believe
that God created human beings from the dust of the earth
and made and formed them in his image and likeness—
  good, just, and holy;
  able by their will to conform
  in all things
  to the will of God.

But when they were in honor
they did not understand it[22]
and did not recognize their excellence.
But they subjected themselves willingly to sin
and consequently to death and the curse,
  lending their ear to the word of the devil.

21. Matt 10:29–30.
22. Ps 49:20.

For they transgressed the commandment of life,
    which they had received,
and by their sin they separated themselves from God,
    who was their true life,
having corrupted their entire nature.

So they made themselves guilty
and subject to physical and spiritual death,
    having become wicked,
    perverse,
    an corrupt in all their ways.

They lost all their excellent gifts
    which they had received from God,
and retained none of them
except for small traces,
    which are enough to make them
    inexcusable.

Moreover, all the light in us is turned to darkness,
as the Scripture teaches us:
    "The light shines in the darkness,
    and the darkness did not overcome it."[23]
Here John calls the human race "darkness."

Therefore we reject everything taught to the contrary
concerning human free will,
since humans are nothing but the slaves of sin
and cannot do a thing
unless it is given them from heaven.[24]

For who can boast of being able
to do anything good by oneself,
since Christ says,
    "No one can come to me

---

23. John 1:5.
24. John 3:27.

unless drawn by the Father who sent me"?[25]

Who can glory in their own will
    when they understand that "the mind that is set on the flesh
    is hostile to God"?[26]
Who can speak of their own knowledge
    in view of the fact that "those who are unspiritual
    do not receive the gifts of God's Spirit"?[27]

In short,
who can produce a single thought,
    knowing that we are not able to think a thing
    about ourselves,
    by ourselves,
    but that "our competence is from God"?[28]

And therefore,
what the apostle says
ought rightly to stand fixed and firm:
    God works within us
    both to will and to do
    according to his good pleasure.[29]

For there is no understanding nor will
conforming to God's understanding and will
apart from Christ's involvement,
    as he teaches us when he says,
    "Apart from me you can do nothing."[30]

ARTICLE 15: THE DOCTRINE OF ORIGINAL SIN

We believe

25. John 6:44.
26. Rom 8:7.
27. 1 Cor 2:14.
28. 2 Cor 3:5.
29. Phil 2:13.
30. John 15:5.

that by the disobedience of Adam
original sin has been spread
through the whole human race.[31]

It is a corruption of the whole human nature—
an inherited depravity which even infects small infants
    in their mother's womb,
and the root which produces in humanity
    every sort of sin.
It is therefore so vile and enormous in God's sight
that it is enough to condemn the human race,
and it is not abolished
    or wholly uprooted
    even by baptism,
        seeing that sin constantly boils forth
        as though from a contaminated spring.

Nevertheless,
it is not imputed to
God's children
for their condemnation
but is forgiven
by his grace and mercy—
    not to put them to sleep
    but so that the awareness of this corruption
    might often make believers groan
    as they long to be set free
    from the body of this death.[32]

Therefore we reject the error of the Pelagians
who say that sin is nothing else than a matter of imitation.

ARTICLE 16: THE DOCTRINE OF ELECTION

We believe that—

31. Rom 5:12–13.
32. Rom 7:24.

all Adam's descendants having thus fallen
into perdition and ruin
by the sin of Adam—
God showed himself to be as he is:
merciful and just.

God is merciful
in withdrawing and saving from this perdition those who,
in eternal and unchangeable divine counsel,
have been elected and chosen in Jesus Christ our Lord
by his pure goodness,
without any consideration of their works.

God is just
in leaving the others in their ruin and fall
into which they plunged themselves.

ARTICLE 17: THE RECOVERY OF FALLEN HUMANITY

We believe that our good God,
by marvelous divine wisdom and goodness,
seeing that Adam and Even had plunged themselves in this manner
into both physical and spiritual death
and made themselves completely miserable,
set out to find them,
though they,
trembling all over,
were fleeing from God.

And God comforted them,
promising to give them his Son,
born of a woman,[33]
to crush the head of the serpent,[34]
and to make them blessed.

33. Gal 4:4.
34. Gen 3:15.

ARTICLE 18: THE INCARNATION

So then we confess
that God fulfilled the promise
 made to the early fathers and mothers
 by the mouth of the holy prophets
when he sent the only and eternal Son of God
into the world
at the time appointed.

The Son took the "form of a slave"
and was made in "human form,"[35]
 truly assuming a real human nature,
 with all its weaknesses,
 except for sin;
 being conceived in the womb of the blessed virgin Mary
 by the power of the Holy Spirit,
 without male participation.

And Christ not only assumed human nature
 as far as the body is concerned
but also a real human soul,
 in order to be a real human being.
for since the soul had been lost as well as the body,
Christ had to assume them both
to save them both together.

Therefore we confess
 (against the heresy of the Anabaptists
 who deny that Christ assumed
 human flesh from his mother)
that Christ shared the very flesh and blood of children;[36]
being the fruit of the loins of David according to the flesh,[37]
descended from David according to the flesh;[38]

35. Phil 2:7.
36. Heb 2:14.
37. Acts 2:30.
38. Rom 1:3.

the fruit of the womb of the virgin Mary;[39]
born of a woman;[40]
the seed of David;[41]
the root of Jesse;[42]
descended from Judah,[43]
    having assumed descent from Abraham and Sarah,
    and was made like his brothers and sisters,
        yet without sin.[44]

In this way Christ is truly our Immanuel—
    that is: "God with us."[45]

ARTICLE 19: THE TWO NATURES OF CHRIST

We believe that by being thus conceived
the person of the Son has been inseparably united
and joined together
with human nature,
    in such a way that there are not two Sons of God,
    nor two persons,
    but two natures united in a single person,
    with each nature retaining its own distinct properties.

Thus his divine nature has always remained uncreated,
    without beginning of days or end of life,[46]
    filling heaven and earth.

Christ's human nature has not lost its properties
but continues to have those of a creature—
    it has a beginning of days;

39. Luke 1:42.
40. Gal 4:4.
41. 2 Tim 2:8.
42. Rom 15:12.
43. Heb 7:14.
44. Heb 2:17; 4:15.
45. Matt 1:23.
46. Heb 7:3.

it is of a finite nature
and retains all that belongs to a real body.
And even though he,
by his resurrection,
gave it immortality,
that nonetheless did not change
the reality of his human nature;
for our salvation and resurrection
depend also on the reality of his body.

But these two natures
are so united together in one person
that they are not even separated by his death.

So then,
what he committed to his Father when he died
as a real human spirit which left his body.
But meanwhile his divine nature remained
united with his human nature
even when he was lying in the grave;
and his deity never ceased to be in him,
just as it was in him when he was a little child,
though for a while it did not so reveal itself.

These are the reasons why we confess him
to be true God and truly human—
true God in order to conquer death
by his power,
and truly human that he might die for us
in the weakness of his flesh.

ARTICLE 20: THE JUSTICE AND MERCY OF GOD IN CHRIST

We believe that God—
who is perfectly merciful
and also very just—
sent the Son to assume the nature

in which the disobedience had been committed,
  in order to bear in it the punishment of sin
  by his most bitter passion and death.

So God made known his justice toward his son,
  who was charged with our sin,
and he poured out his goodness and mercy on us,
  who are guilty and worthy of damnation,
giving to us his Son to die,
  by a most perfect love,
and raising him to life
  for our justification,
      in order that by him
      we might have immortality
      and eternal life.

ARTICLE 21: THE ATONEMENT

We believe
that Jesus Christ is a high priest forever
according to the order of Melchizedek—
  made such by an oath—
and that he presented himself
in our name
before his Father,
to appease his Father's wrath
with full satisfaction
  by offering himself
      on the tree of the cross
  and pouring out his precious blood
      for the cleansing of our sins,
      as the prophets had predicted.

For it is written
that "the punishment that made us whole"
was placed on the Son of God
and that "by his bruises we are healed."
He was "like a lamb that is led to the slaughter;"

he was "numbered with the transgressors"[47]
and condemned as a criminal by Pontius Pilate,
    though Pilate had declared
    that he was innocent.

So he paid back
what he had not stolen,[48]
and he suffered
    "the righteous for the unrighteous,"[49]
    in both his body and his soul—
in such a way that
when he sensed the horrible punishment
required by our sins
"his sweat became like great drops of blood
falling down on the ground."[50]
He cried, "My God, my God,
why have you forsaken me?"[51]

And he endured all this
for the forgiveness of our sins.

Therefore we rightly say with Paul that
we know nothing "except Jesus Christ, and him crucified";[52]
we "regard everything as loss
because of the surpassing value
of knowing Christ Jesus [our] Lord."[53]
We find all comforts in his wounds
and have no need to seek or invent any other means
to reconciled ourselves with God
than this one and only sacrifice,
once made,

47. Isa 53:4–12.
48. Ps 69:4.
49. 1 Pet 3:18.
50. Luke 22:44.
51. Matt 27:46.
52. 1 Cor 2:2.
53. Phil 3:8.

which renders believers perfect
forever.

This is also why
the angel of God called him Jesus—
that is, "Savior"—
    because he would save his people
    from their sins.[54]

ARTICLE 22: THE RIGHTEOUSNESS OF FAITH

We believe that
for us to acquire true knowledge of this great mystery
the Holy Spirit kindles in our hearts a true faith
that embraces Jesus Christ,
    with all his merits,
and makes him its own
and no longer looks for anything
    apart from him.

For it must necessarily follow
that either all that is required for our salvation
is not in Christ or,
if all is in him,
then those who have Christ by faith
have his salvation entirely.

Therefore,
to say that Christ is not enough
but that something else is needed as well
is a most enormous blasphemy against God—
    for it would then follow
    that Jesus Christ is only half a Savior.
And therefore we justly say with Paul
that we are justified "by faith alone"
or "by faith apart from works."[55]

54. Matt 1:21.
55. Rom 3:28.

However,
we do not mean,
properly speaking,
that it is faith itself that justifies us—
    for faith is only the instrument
    by which we embrace Christ,
    our righteousness

But Jesus Christ is our righteousness
    in making available to us all his merits
    and all the holy works he has done
    for us and in our place.
And faith is the instrument
    that keeps us in communion with him
    and with all his benefits.

When those benefits are made ours,
they are more than enough to absolve us
of our sins.

ARTICLE 23: THE JUSTIFICATION OF SINNERS

We believe
that our blessedness lies in the forgiveness of our sins
because of Jesus Christ,
and that in it our righteousness before God is contained,
    as David and Paul teach us
    when they declare those people blessed
    to whom God grants righteousness
    apart from works.[56]

And the same apostle says
that we are "justified by his grace as a gift,
through the redemption that is in Christ Jesus."[57]
And therefore we cling to this foundation,

56. Ps 32:1; Rom 4:6.
57. Rom 3:24.

which is firm forever,
> giving all glory to God,
> humbling ourselves,
> and recognizing ourselves as we are;
> not claiming a thing for ourselves or our merits
> and leaning and resting
>> on sole obedience of Christ crucified,
>> which is ours when we believe in him.

That is enough to cover all our sins
and to make us confident
freeing the conscience from the fear, dread, and terror
> of God's approach,
without doing what our first parents, Adam and Eve, did,
> who trembled as they tried to cover themselves
>> with fig leaves.

In fact,
if we had to appear before God relying—
> no matter how little—
on ourselves or some other creature,
then, alas, we would be swallowed up.

Therefore everyone must say with David:
"[Lord] do not enter into judgment with your servant,
> for no one living is righteous before you."[58]

ARTICLE 24: THE SANCTIFICATION OF SINNERS

We believe that this true faith,
> produced in us by the hearing of God's Word
> and by the work of the Holy Spirit,
regenerates us and makes us new creatures,[59]
> causing us to live a new life[60]
> and freeing us from the slavery of sin.

---

58. Ps 143:2.
59. 2 Cor 5:17.
60. Rom 6:4.

Therefore,
far from making people cold
toward living in a pious and holy way,
this justifying faith,
quite to the contrary,
so works within them that
    apart from it
they will never do a thing out of love for God
but only out of love for themselves
and fear of being condemned.

So then, it is impossible
for this holy faith to be unfruitful in a human being,
seeing that we do not speak of an empty faith
but of what Scripture calls
"faith working through love,"[61]
    which moves people to do by themselves
    the works that God has commanded
        in the Word.

Those works,
    proceeding from the good root of faith,
are good and acceptable to God,
    since they are all sanctified by God's grace.
Yet they do not count toward our justification—
    for by faith in Christ we are justified,
    even before we do good works.
        Otherwise they could not be good,
        any more than the fruit of a tree could be good
        if the tree is not good in the first place.

So then, we do good works,
but not for merit—
    for what would we merit?
Rather, we are indebted to God for the good works we do,
    and not God to us,

61. Gal 5:6.

since God "is at work in [us], enabling [us] both
    to will and to work for his good pleasure"[62]—
thus keeping in mind what is written:
    "When you have done all that you were ordered to do,
    say, 'We are worthless slaves;
    we have done only what we ought to have done.'"[63]

Yet we do not wish to deny
that God rewards good works—
but it is by grace
that God crowns these gifts.

Moreover,
although we do good works
we do not base our salvation on them
    for we cannot do any work
    that is not defiled by our flesh
    and also worthy of punishment.
And even if we could point to one,
    memory of a single sin is enough
    for God to reject that work.

So we would always be in doubt,
    tossed back and forth
    without any certainty,
and our poor consciences would be tormented constantly
    if they did not rest on the merit
    of suffering and death of our Savior.

ARTICLE 25: THE FULFILLMENT OF THE LAW

We believe
that the ceremonies and symbols of the law have ended
    with the coming of Christ,
and that all foreshadowings have come to an end,
so that the use of them ought to be abolished

62. Phil 2:13.
63. Luke 17:10.

among Christians.
Yet the truth and substance of these things
remain for us in Jesus Christ,
 in whom they have been fulfilled.

Nevertheless,
we continue to use the witnesses
drawn from the law and prophets
 to confirm us in the gospel
  and to regulate our lives with full integrity
   for the glory of God,
    according to the will of God.

ARTICLE 26: THE INTERCESSION OF CHRIST

We believe that we have no access to God
except through the one and only Mediator and Intercessor,
"Jesus Christ the righteous,"[64]
who
therefore was made human
uniting together the divine and human natures,
so that we human beings might have access to the divine Majesty.
Otherwise we would have no access.

But this Mediator,
 whom the Father has appointed between himself and us,
ought not terrify us by his greatness,
 so that we have to look for another one,
 according to our fancy.
For neither in heaven nor among the creatures on earth
is there anyone who loves us
more than Jesus Christ does.
 Although he was "in the form of God,"
 Christ nevertheless "emptied himself,"
 taking "human form" and "the form of a slave" for us;[65]
 and he made himself "like his brothers and sisters

64. 1 John 2:1.
65. Phil 2:6–8.

in every respect."[66]

Suppose we had to find another intercessor.
> Who would love us more than he who gave his life for us,
> even though "we were his enemies"?[67]
And suppose we had to find one who has prestige and power.
> Who has as much of these as he who is seated
> > at the right hand of the Father,[68]
> and who has "all authority
> > in heaven and on earth:?[69]
> And who will be heard more readily
> > than God's own dearly beloved Son?

So, the practice of honoring the saints as intercessors
in fact dishonors them
because of its misplaced faith.
That was something the saints never did nor asked for,
but which in keeping with their duty,
> as appears from their writings,
they consistently refused.

We should not plead here
that we are unworthy—
> for it is not a question of offering our prayers
> on the basis of our own dignity
> but only on the basis of the excellence and dignity
> of Jesus Christ,
> > whose righteousness is ours by faith.

Since the apostle for good reason
wants us to get rid of this foolish fear—
> or rather, this unbelief—
he says to us that Jesus Christ
was made like "his brothers and sisters in every respect,

66. Heb 2:17.
67. Rom 5:10.
68. Rom 8:34; Heb 13.
69. Matt 28:18.

so that he might be a merciful and faithful high priest"
to purify the sins of the people.[70]
For since he suffered,
being tempted,
he is also able to help those
who are tempted.[71]

And further,
to encourage us more
to approach him
he says,
"Since then, we have a great high priest
who has passed through the heavens,
Jesus, the Son of God,
let us hold fast to our confession.
For we do not have a high priest
who is unable to sympathize with our weaknesses,
but we have one who in every respect has been tested
as we are,
yet without sin.
Let us therefore approach
the throne of grace
with boldness,
so that we may receive mercy
and find grace
to help in time of need."[72]

The same apostle says that
we "have confidence to enter the sanctuary
by the blood of Jesus."
"Let us approach with a true heart
in full assurance of faith . . ."[73]

Likewise,

70. Heb 2:17.
71. Heb 2:18.
72. Heb 4:14–16.
73. Heb 10:19, 22.

Christ "holds his priesthood permanently . . . .
Consequently, he is able for all time to save
those who approach God through him,
since he always lives
to make intercession for them."[74]
What more do we need?
For Christ himself declares:
"I am the way, and the truth, and the life.
No one comes to the Father
except through me."[75]
Why should we seek another intercessor?

Since it has pleased God
to give us the Son as our Intercessor,
let us not leave him for another—
        or rather seek, without ever finding,
For when giving Christ to us,
God knew well that we were sinners.

Therefore,
in following the command of Christ
we call on the heavenly Father
through Christ,
our only Mediator,
As we are taught by the Lord's Prayer,
        being assured that we shall obtain
        all we ask of the Father
        in his name.

ARTICLE 27: THE HOLY CATHOLIC CHURCH

We believe and confess
one single catholic or universal church—
        a holy congregation and gathering
        of true Christian believers
                awaiting their entire salvation in Jesus Crist,

74. Heb 7:24–25.
75. John 14:6.

being washed by his blood,
and sanctified and sealed by the Holy Spirit.

This church has existed from the beginning of the world
and will last until the end,
> as appears from the fact
> that Christ is eternal King
> who cannot be without subjects.

And this holy church is preserved by God
against the rage of the whole world,
> even though for a time
> it may appear very small
> to human eyes—
> as though it were snuffed out.

For example,
during the very dangerous time of Ahab
the Lord preserved for himself seven thousand
who did not bend their knees to Baal.[76]

And so this holy church
is not confined,
bound,
or limited to a certain place or certain people.

But it is spread and dispersed
throughout the entire world,
> though still joined and united
>> in heart and will,
>> in one and the same Spirit,
>> by the power of faith.

ARTICLE 28: THE OBLIGATIONS OF CHURCH MEMBERS

We believe that
> since this holy assembly and congregation

76. 1 Kgs 19:18.

is the gathering of those who are saved
and there is no salvation apart from it,
people ought not to withdraw from it,
content to be by themselves,
regardless of their status or condition.

But all people are obliged
to join and unite with it,
keeping the unity of the church
by submitting to tis instruction and discipline,
by bending their necks under the yoke of Jesus Christ,
and by serving to build up one another,
according to the gifts God has given them
as members of each other
in the same body.

And to preserve this unity more effectively,
it is the duty of all believers,
according to God's Word,
to separate themselves
from those who do not belong to the church
in order to join this assembly
wherever God has established it,
even if civil authorities and royal decrees forbid
and death and physical punishment result.

And so,
all who withdraw from the church
or do not join it
act contrary to God's ordinance.

ARTICLE 29: THE MARKS OF THE TRUE CHURCH

We believe that we ought to discern
diligently and very carefully,
by the Word of God,
what is the true church—
for all sects in the world today

claim for themselves the name of "the church."

We are not speaking here of the company of hypocrites
who are mixed among the good in the church
and who nonetheless are not part of it,
even though they are physically there.
But we are speaking of distinguishing
the body and fellowship of the true church
from all sects that call themselves "the church."

The true church can be recognized
if it has the following marks:
    The church engages in the pure preaching
        of the gospel;
    it makes use of the pure administration of the sacraments
        as Christ instituted them;
    it practices church discipline
        for correcting faults.

In short, it governs itself
according to the pure Word of God,
    rejecting all things contrary to it
    and holding Jesus Christ as the only Head.
By these marks one can be assured
of recognizing the true church—
    and no one ought to be separated from it.

As for those who can belong to the church.
we can recognize them by the distinguishing marks of Christians:
    namely by faith,
    and by their fleeing from sin and pursuing righteousness,
        once they have received the one and only Savior,
        Jesus Christ.

They love the true God and their neighbors,
    without turning to the right or left,
and they crucify the flesh and its works.

Though great weakness remains in them,
they fight against it
by the Spirit
all the days of their lives,
appealing constantly
to the blood, suffering, death, and obedience of the Lord Jesus,
    in whom they have forgiveness of their sins,
    through faith in him.

As for the false church,
it assigns more authority to itself and its ordinances
    than to the Word of God;
it does not want to subject itself
    to the yoke of Christ;
it does not administer the sacraments;
    as Christ commanded in his Word;
it rather adds to them or subtracts from them
    as it pleases;
it bases itself on humans,
    more than on Jesus Christ;
it persecutes those
    who live holy lives according to the Word of God
    and who rebuke it for its faults, greed, and idolatry.

These two churches
are easy to recognize
and thus to distinguish
from each other.

ARTICLE 30: THE GOVERNMENT OF THE CHURCH

We believe that this true church
ought to be governed according to the spiritual order
that our Lord has taught us in his Word.
    There should be ministers or pastors
        to preach the Word of God
        and administer the sacraments.
    There should also be elders and deacons,

  along with the pastors,
  to make up the council of the church.

By this means
true religion is preserved;
true doctrine is able to take its course;
and evil people are corrected spiritually and held in check,
  so that also the poor
  and all the afflicted
  may be helped and comforted
  according to their need.

By this means
everything will be done well
and in good order
in the church,
  when such persons are elected
  who are faithful
  and are chosen according to the rule
  that Paul gave Timothy.[77]

ARTICLE 31: THE OFFICERS OF THE CHURCH

We believe that
ministers of the Word of God, elders, and deacons
ought to be chosen to their offices
by a legitimate election of the church,
with prayer in the name of the Lord,
and in good order,
  as the Word of God teaches.

So all must be careful
not to push themselves forward improperly,
but must wait for God's call,
  so that they ma be assured of their calling
  and be certain that they are
  chosen by the Lord.

77. 1 Tim 3.

As for the ministers of the Word,
they all have the same power and authority,
    no matter where they may be,
since they are all servants of Jesus Christ,
    the only universal bishop,
    and the only head of the church.

Moreover,
to keep God's holy order
from being violated or despised,
we say that everyone ought,
as much as possible,
to hold the ministers of the Word and elders of the church
in special esteem,
    because of the work they do,
and be at peace with them,
    without grumbling, quarreling, or fighting.

ARTICLE 32: THE ORDER AND DISCIPLINE OF THE CHURCH

We also believe that
    although it is useful and good
for whose who govern the churches
to establish and set up
a certain order among themselves
for maintaining the body of the church,
they ought always to guard against deviating
from what Christ,
our only Master,
has ordained
for us.

Therefore we reject all human innovations
and all laws imposed on us,
in our worship of God,
which bind and force our consciences

in any way.

So we accept only what is proper
to maintain harmony and unity
and to keep all in obedience
to God.

To that end excommunication,
with all it involves,
according to the Word of God,
is required.

ARTICLE 33: THE SACRAMENTS

We believe that our good God,
mindful of our crudeness and weakness,
has ordained sacraments for us
    to seal his promises in us,
      to pledge good will and grace toward us,
      and also to nourish and sustain our faith.

God has added these to the Word of the gospel
to represent better to our external senses
both what God enables us to understand by the Word
and what he does inwardly in our hearts,
    confirming in us
    the salvation he imparts to us.

For they are visible signs and seals
of something internal and invisible.
    by means of which God works in us
    through the power of the Holy Spirit.
So they are not empty and hollow signs
to fool and deceive us,
    for their truth is Jesus Christ,
    without whom they would be nothing.

Moreover,

we are satisfied with the number of sacraments
that Christ our Master has ordained for us.
There are only two:
    the sacrament of baptism
    and the Holy Supper of Jesus Christ.

ARTICLE 34: THE SACRAMENT OF BAPTISM

We believe and confess that Jesus Christ,
in whom the law is fulfilled,
has by his shed blood
put an end to every other shedding of blood,
    which anyone might do or wish to do
    in order to atone or satisfy for sins.

Having abolished circumcision,
which was done with blood,
Christ established in its place
the sacrament of baptism.

    By it we are received into Gods church
        and set apart from all other people and alien religions,
    that we may wholly belong to him
        whose mark and sign we bear.
    Baptism also witnesses to us
    that God, being our gracious Father,
        will be our God forever.

Therefore Christ has commanded
that all those who belong to him
be baptized with pure water
    "in the name of the Father
    and of the Son
    and of the Holy Spirit."[78]

In this way God signifies to us
that just as water washes away the dirt of the body

78. Matt 28:19.

when it is poured on us
and also is seen on the bodies of those who are baptized
when it is sprinkled on them,
so too the blood of Christ does the same thing internally,
in the soul,
by the Holy Spirit.

> It washes and cleanses it from its sins
> and transforms us from being the children of wrath
> into the children of God.

This does not happen by the physical water
but by the sprinkling of the precious blood of the Son of God,
who is our Red Sea,
through which we must pass
> to escape the tyranny of Pharaoh,
> > who is the devil
> and to enter the spiritual land
> > of Canaan.

So ministers,
as far as their work is concerned,
give us the sacrament and what is visible,
but our Lord gives what the sacrament signifies—
namely the invisible gifts and graces;
> washing, purifying, and cleansing our souls
> > of all filth and unrighteousness;
> renewing our hearts and filling them
> > with all comfort;
> giving us true assurance
> > of his fatherly goodness;
> clothing us with the "new self"
> > and stripping off the "old self"
> > with its practices."[79]

For this reason we believe that
anyone who aspires to reach eternal life

79. Col 3:9–10.

ought to be baptized only once
without ever repeating it—
for we cannot be born twice.
Yet this baptism is profitable
not only when the water is no us
and when we receive it
but throughout our
entire lives.

For that reason we reject the error of the Anabaptists
    who are not content with a single baptism
        once received
    and also condemn the baptism
        of the children of believers.
    We believe our children ought to be baptized
    and sealed with the sign of the covenant,
        as little children were circumcised in Israel
        on the basis of the same promises
        made to our children.

And truly,
Christ has shed his blood no less
for washing the little children of believers
than he did for adults.

Therefore they ought to receive the sign and sacrament
of what Christ has done for them,
    just as the Lord commanded in the law that
    by offering a lamb for them
    the sacrament of the suffering and death of Christ
    would be granted them
    shortly after their birth.
    This was the sacrament of Jesus Christ.

Furthermore,
baptism does for our children
what circumcision did for the Jewish people.
That is why Paul calls baptism

the "circumcision of Christ."[80]

ARTICLE 35: THE SACRAMENT OF THE LORD'S SUPPER

We believe and confess
that our Savor Jesus Christ
has ordained and instituted the sacrament of the Holy Super
to nourish and sustain those
who are already regenerated and ingrafted
into his family,
which is his church.

Now those who are born again have two lives in them.
The one is physical and temporal—
    they have it from the moment of their first birth,
    and it is common to all.
The other is spiritual and heavenly,
    and is given them in their second birth—
    it comes through the Word of the gospel
    in the communion of the body of Christ;
    and this life is common to God's elect only.

Thus, to support the physical and earthly life
God has prescribed for us
an appropriate earthly and material bread,
which is as common to all people
as life itself.
But to maintain the spiritual and heavenly life
that belongs to believers,
God has sent a living bread
that came down from heaven:
namely Jesus Christ,
    who nourishes and maintains
    the spiritual life of believers
    when eaten—
    that is, when appropriated
    and received spiritually

80. Col 2:11.

by faith.

To represent to us
this spiritual and heavenly bread
Christ has instituted
an earthly and visible bread as the sacrament of his body
and wine as the sacrament of his blood.
He did this to testify to us that
just as truly as we take and hold the sacrament in our hands
and eat and drink it with our mouths,
    by which our life is then sustained,
so truly we receive into our souls
    for our spiritual life,
    the true body and true blood of Christ,
    our only Savior.
We receive these by faith,
    which is the hand and mouth of our souls.

Now it is certain
that Jesus Christ did not prescribe
his sacraments for us in vain,
since he works in us all he represents
by these holy signs,
    although the manner in which he does it
    goes beyond our understanding
    and is incomprehensible to us,
        just as the operation of God's Spirit
        is hidden and incomprehensible.

Yet we do not go wrong when we say
that what is eaten is Christ's own natural body
and what is drunk is his own blood—
but the manner in which we eat it
is not by the mouth, but by the Spirit
through faith.

In that way Jesus Christ remains always seated
at the right hand of God the Father

in heaven—
but he never refrains on that account
to communicate himself to us
through faith.
This banquet is a spiritual table
at which Christ communicates himself to us
with all his benefits.
At that table he makes us enjoy himself
as much as the merits of his suffering and death,
as he nourishes, strengthens, and comforts
our poor, desolate souls
    by the eating of his flesh,
and relieves and renews them
    by the drinking of his blood.

Moreover,
though the sacraments and what they signify are joined together,
not all receive both of them.
The wicked certainly take the sacrament,
to their condemnation,
but do not receive the truth of the sacrament,
    just as Judas and Simon the Sorcerer both indeed
    received the sacrament,
    but not Christ,
    who was signified by it.
    He is communicated only to believers.

Finally,
with humility and reverence
we receive the holy sacrament
in the gathering of God's people,
    as we engage together,
    with thanksgiving,
    in a holy remembrance
    of the death of Christ our Savior,
    and as we thus confess
    our faith and Christian religion.
Therefore none should come to this table

without examining themselves carefully,
> lest by eating this bread
> and drinking this cup
> they "eat and drink judgment against themselves."[81]

In short,
by the use of this holy sacrament
we are moved to a fervent love
of God and our neighbors.

Therefore we reject
as desecrations of the sacraments
all the muddled ideas and condemnable inventions
that people have added and mixed in with them.
And we say that we should be content with the procedure
that Christ and the apostles have taught us
and speak of these things
as they have spoken of them.

ARTICLE 36: THE CIVIL GOVERNMENT

We believe that
because of the depravity of the human race,
our good God has ordained kings, princes, and civil officers.
God wants the world to be governed by laws and policies
so that human lawlessness may be restrained
and that everything may be conducted in good order
among human beings.

For that purpose God has placed the sword
in the hands of the government,
to punish evil people
and protect the good.

[*RCA only*[82]

---

81. 1 Cor 11:29.

82. The Reformed Church in America retains the original full text, choosing to recognize that the confession was written within a historical context which may not accurately

And the government's task is not limited
to caring for and watching over the public domain
but extends also to upholding the sacred ministry,
 with a view to removing and destroying
  all idolatry and false worship of the Antichrist;
 to promoting the kingdom of Jesus Christ;
 and to furthering the preaching of the gospel everywhere;
 to the end that God may be honored and served by everyone,
 as he requires in his Word.]

[*CRC only*[83]
And being called in this manner
to contribute to the advancement of a society
that is pleasing to God,
the civil rulers have the task,
 subject to God's law,
of removing every obstacle
 to the preaching of the gospel
 and to every aspect of divine worship.

They should do this
while completely refraining from every tendency
 toward exercising absolute authority,
and while functioning in the sphere entrusted to them,
 with the means belonging to them.

They should do it in order that
 the word of God may have free course;
 the kingdom of Jesus Christ may make progress;
 and every anti-Christian power may be resisted.]

Moreover everyone,
regardless of status, condition, or rank,
must be subject to the government,
and pay taxes,

---

describe the situation that pertains today.

83. Synod 1958 of the Christian Reformed Church replaced the aforementioned paragraph with the following three paragraphs (in brackets).

and hold its representatives in honor and respect,
and obey them in all things that are not in conflict
    with God's Word,
praying for them
    that the Lord may be willing to lead them
        in all their ways
    and that we may live a peaceful and quiet life
        in all piety and decency.

[(*RCA only*[84]
And on this matter we reject the Anabaptists, anarchists,
and in general all those who want
to reject the authorities and civil officers
and to subvert justice
    by introducing common ownership of goods
    and corrupting the moral order
        that God has established among human beings.]

ARTICLE 37: THE LAST JUDGMENT

Finally we believe,
according to God's Word,
that when the time appointed by the Lord is come
(which is unknown to all creatures)
and the number of the elect is complete,
our Lord Jesus Christ will come from heaven,
    bodily and visibly,
as he ascended,
    with glory and majesty,
to declare himself the judge
    of the living and the dead.
He will burn this old world,
    in fire and flame,
    in order to cleanse it.

---

84. The RCA retains this final paragraph of the original Article 36, choosing to recognize that the confession was written within a historical context which may not accurately describe the situation that pertains today. Synod 158 of the CRC directed that this paragraph be taken from the body of the text and placed in a footnote.

Then all human creatures will appear in person
before the great judge—
    men, women, and children,
    who have lived from the beginning until the end
    of the world.
They will be summoned there
"with the archangel's call
and with the sound of God's trumpet."[85]

For all those who died before that time
will be raised from the earth,
    their spirits being joined and united
    with their own bodies
    in which they lived.
And as for those who are still alive,
they will not die like the others
but will be changed "in the twinkling of an eye"
from perishable to imperishable.[86]

Then the books (that is the consciences) will be opened,
and the dead will be judged
    according to the things they did in the world,[87]
    whether good or evil.
Indeed, all people will give account
of all the idle words they have spoken,[88]
    which the world regards
    as only playing games.
And then the secretes and hypocrisies of all people
will be publicly uncovered
in the sight of all.

Therefore,
with good reason

    85. 1 Thess 4:16.
    86. 1 Cor 15: 51–53.
    87. Rev 20:12.
    88. Matt 12:36.

the thought of this judgment
is horrible and dreadful
to wicked and evil people.
But it is very pleasant
and a great comfort
to the righteous and elect,
 since their total redemption
 will then be accomplished.
They will then receive the fruits of their labor
 and of the trouble they have suffered;
their innocence will be openly recognized by all;
and they will see the terrible vengeance
 that God will bring on the evil ones
 who tyrannized, oppressed, and tormented them
 in this world.

The evil ones will be convicted
 by the witness of their own consciences,
and shall be made immortal—
 but only to be tormented
 in "the eternal fire
 prepared for the devil and his angels."[89]

In contrast,
the faithful and elect will be crowned
 with glory and honor.
The Son of God will profess their names[90]
 before God his Father and the holy and elect angels;
all tears will be wiped from their eyes;[91]
and their cause—
 at present condemned as heretical and evil
 by many judges and civil officers—
will be acknowledged as the cause of the Son of God.

And as a gracious reward

89. Matt 25:41.
90. Matt 10:32.
91. Rev 7:17.

the Lord will make them possess a glory
such as the human heart
could never imagine.

So we look forward to that great day with longing
in order to enjoy fully
the promises of God in Christ Jesus,
our Lord.

BIBLIOGRAPHY

Abbott, Walter M., editor. *The Documents of Vatican II*. New York: America Press, 1966.

The Acts and Proceedings of the 172th Regular Session of the General Synod. Vol. 63. Reformed Church in America, 1978.

Aulèn, Gustav. *Christus Victor: An Historical Study of the Three Main Types of the Idea of Atonement*. Translated by A. G. Herbert. New York: Macmillan, 1961.

Barth, Karl. *Church Dogmatics IV.1*. Translated by G. W. Bromiley. Edinburgh: T. & T. Clark, 1956.

———. *Church Dogmatics IV.3.2*. Translated by G. W. Bromiley. Edinburgh: T. & T. Clark, 1962.

———. *Theology and Church: Shorter Writings*. London: SCM, 1962.

Beek, Abraham van de. *Jezus kurios: Christologie als hart van de theologie*. Kampen: Kok, 1998.

"Belgic Confession." In *Creeds of Christendom*, edited by Philip Schaff, 3:383–436. Grand Rapids: Baker, 1977.

Berger, Peter. *The Sacred Canopy: Elements of a Sociological Theory of Religion*. Garden City, NY: Anchor, 1969.

Berkhof, Hendrikus. *Christ and the Powers*. Translated by John H. Yoder. Scottsdale, PA: Herald, 1962.

———. "De apostoliciteit der kerk." *Nederlands Theologische Tijdschrift* 2:3 & 4, (1948).

———. *Well-Founded Hope*. Richmond: John Knox, 1969.

Berkouwer, G. K. *The Church*. Translated by James E. Davison. Grand Rapids: Eerdmans, 1967.

Billings, J. Todd. "Rediscovering the Catholic-Reformed Tradition Today." In *Reformed Catholicity: The Promise of Retrieval for Theology and Biblical Interpretation*, by Michael Allen and Scott R. Swain, 143–61. Grand Rapids: Baker Academic, 2015.

———. *Union with Christ: Reframing Theology and Ministry for the Church*. Grand Rapids: Baker Academic, 2011.

Bloom, Harold. *The American Religion*. New York: Hartley, 2013.

The Book of Church Order. New York: Reformed Church, 2014.

The Book of Confessions: Study Edition. Part 1 of the Constitution of the Presbyterian Church (U.S.A.). Louisville: Geneva, 1966.

Calvin, John. *Institutes of the Christian Religion*. 2 vols. Translated by Ford Lewis Battles. Philadelphia: Westminster, 1960.

————. "Short Treatise on the Holy Supper of Our Lord and Only Saviour Jesus Christ." In *Calvin's Theological Treatises*, edited by J. K. S. Reid, 140–66. Philadelphia: Westminster, 1954.

Chantepie de la Saussaye, Daniel, Sr. "Leven en rigting." In *Verzameld Werk*, 3:11–149. Zoetermeer: Boekencentrum, 2003.

Evenhuis, R. B. *Ook dat was Amsterdam*. Vol. 1. Amsterdam: Ten Have, 1965.

Foundations and Perspectives of Confession. Netherlands Reformed Church. New Brunswick, NJ: New Brunswick Theological Seminary, 1955.

Girard, Renè. *Things Hidden Since the Foundation of the World*. Translated by Stephen Bann and Michael Metteer. Stanford, CA: Stanford University, 1987.

Gootjes, Nicholas H. *The Belgic Confession: Its History and Sources*. Grand Rapids: Baker Academic, 2007.

Gunton, Colin. *Actuality of the Atonement: A Study of Metaphor, Rationality and the Christian Tradition*. Edinburgh: T. & T. Clark, 1988.

Hall, Douglas John. *Confessing the Faith: Christian Theology in a North American Context*. Minneapolis: Fortress, 1996.

————. *Professing the Faith*. Minneapolis: Fortress, 1993.

————. *Thinking the Faith*. Minneapolis: Fortress, 1989.

Heschel, Abraham. *Man Is Not Alone: A Philosophy of Religion*. New York: Ferrar, Strauss & Giroux, 1951.

Heppe, Heinrich. *Reformed Dogmatics: Set Out and Illustrated from the Sources*. Grand Rapids: Baker, 1950.

"Joint Declaration on the Doctrine of Justification." Luther World Church and Roman Catholic Church. http://www.vatican.va/roman_curia/pontifical_councils/chrstuni/documents/rc_pc_chrstuni_doc_31101999_cath-luth-joint-declaration_en.html.

Kemps, Marvin, translator. "Guido de Brès's Letter to Philip II of Spain." www.dprf.co.uk/debresletter.htm#VdSzx_Viko.

Kerkorde der Nederlandse Hervormde Kerk. Gravenhage: Boekencentrum, 1969.

Koopmans, J. *De Nederlandse Geloofbelijdenis*. 3rd ed. Amsterdam: Holland, 1939.

Küng, Hans. *The Church*. New York: Sheed & Ward, 1967.

Marsden, George M. *Fundamentalism and American Culture: The Shaping of Twentieth-Century Evangelicalism*. Oxford: Oxford University, 1980.

McEwan, Ian. *Atonement*. New York: Anchor, 2001.

Milbank, John, and Slavoj Žižek. *The Monstrosity of Christ*. Cambridge, MA: MIT, 2009.

Miskotte, K. H. *De kern van de zaak*. Nijkerk: Callenbach, 1950.

————. *Edda en thora: Een vergelijking van Germuanse en Israëalitise religie*. 2nd ed. Nijkekrk: Callenbach, 1970.

————. *When the Gods Are Silent*. Translated by John W. Doberstein. New York: Harper & Row, 1967.

Moltmann, Jürgen. *The Crucified God: The Cross of Christ as the Foundation and Criticism of Christian Theology*. Translated by R. A. Wilson and John Bowden. New York: Harper & Row, 1974.

————. *Theology of Hope: On the Ground and Implications of a Christian Eschatology*. Translated by John W. Leitch. New York: Harper & Row, 1967.

Naudé, Piet J. *Neither Calendar nor Clock: Perspectives on the Belhar Confession*. Grand Rapids: Eerdmans, 2010.

Noordmans, O. "Beginselen van kerkorde." In *Verzameld Werk*, 5:172–245. Kampen: Kok, 1984.

————. *Het koninkrijk der hemelen.* Nijkerk: Callenbach, 1949.

————. "Schrift en belijdenis." In *Verzamelde Werk*, 2:349–353. Kampen: Kok, 1979.

Northcott, Michael S. *A Political Theology of Climate Change.* Grand Rapids: Eerdmans, 2013.

O'Siadhall, Micheal. *The Gossamer Wall: Poems in Witness to the Holocaust.* St. Louis: Time Being, 2002.

Osterhaven, M. Eugene. *Our Confession of Faith: A Study Manual on the Belgic Confession.* Grand Rapids, Baker, 1964.

Our Faith: Ecumenical Creeds, Reformed Confessions, and Other Resources. Grand Rapids, Faith Alive, 2013.

"Our Song of Hope." In *Our Faith: Ecumenical Creeds, Reformed Confessions, and Other Resources.* Christian Reformed Church in North America and Reformed Church in America. Grand Rapids: Faith Alive: 2013.

Polman, A. D. R. *Onze Nederlandse Geloofbelijdenis.* 4 vols. Franker: T. Wever, n.d.

Rosenstock-Huessy, Eugen. *Speech and Reality.* Norwich, CT: Argo, 1970.

Ruler, Arnold Albert van. "De iustificatione." In *Verzameld Werk*, edited by D. van Keulen, 4B:163–235. Zoetermeer: Boekencentrum, 2011.

————. "De reformatische visie op de mens." In *Verzameld Werk*, edited by D. van Keulen, 3:2343–56. Zoetermeer: Boekencentrum. 2009.

————. *Een leven een feest.* Nijkerk: Callenbach, 1972.

————. "Gods voorzienigheid." in *Verzameld Werk*, edited by D. van Keulen, 3:130–132. Zoetermeer: Boekencentrum, 2009.

————. *Heb moed voor de wereld.* Nijkerk: Callenbach, 1953.

————. *Ik geloof.* 7th ed. Nijkerk: Callenbach, n.d.

————. "Leer van de uitverkiezing." In *Verzameld Werk 4-A*, edited by, D. van Keulen, 4A:492–742. Zoetermeer: Boekencentrum, 2011.

————. "Plaats en belijdenis der kerk." In *Visie en Vaart*, 50–137. Holland: Amsterdam, 1947.

————. "Rechtvaarding." In *Verzameld Werk*, edited by D. van Keulen, 4B:158–62. Zoetermeer: Boekencentrum, 2011.

————. "Schiftgezag en kerk." In *Verzameld Werk*, edited by. D. van Keulen, 2:316–34. Zoetermeer: Boekencentrum, 2008.

————. "Ultra-gereformeerde en vrijzinnige." In *Theologishe Werk*, 3:98–163. Nijkerk: Callenbach, 1971.

————. "Vormen en omgang met de bijbel." In *Verzameld Werk*, edited by D. van Keulen, 2:335–62. Zoetermeer: Boekencentrum, 2008.

————. *Der vervulling van de wet.* Nijkerk: Callenbach, 1947.

Rutledge, Fleming. *The Crucifixion: Understanding the Death of Jesus Christ.* Grand Rapids: Eerdmans, 2015.

Seeburg, Reinhold. *Lehrbuch der Dogmengeschichte.* Vol. 3. 5th ed. Basel: Benno Schwab, 1953.

Small, Joseph. "The Church's Conversation with the Confessions." In *Conversation with Confessions: Dialogue in the Reformed Tradition*, edited by Joseph D. Small, 1–15. Louisville: Geneva, 2005.

Smit, D. J. "What Does Status Confessionis Mean?" In *A Moment of Truth: The Confession of the Dutch Reformed Mission Church*, edited by G. D. Cloete and D. J. Smit, 7–32. Grand Rapids: Eerdmans, 1984.

Smith, James K. A. *Desiring the Kingdom: Worship, Worldview, and Cultural Formation.* Grand Rapids: Baker Academic, 2009.

Taylor, Charles. *A Secular Age.* Cambridge, MA: Belnap, 2007.

Torrance, Thomas F. *Theology in Reconstruction.* Grand Rapids: Eerdmans, 1965.

Verboom, W. *Kostbaar belijdenis: De theologie van de Nederlandse Geloofbelijdenis* Zoetermeer: Boekencentrum, 1999.

Vischer, Lukas. "Communion: Responding to God's Gift." In *The Unity of the Church: A Theological State of the Art and Beyond,* edited by Eduardus van der Borght, 19–32. Leiden: Brill, 2010.

Weinrich, Michael. "The Openness and Worldliness of the Church." *In Reformed Theology: Identity and Ecumenicity,* edited by Wallace Alston Jr. and Michael Welker, 412–434. Grand Rapids: Eerdmans, 2003.

White, Lynn, Jr. "The Historical Roots of Our Ecological Crisis." *Science* 155 (1967) 1203–7.

Wink, Walter. *Unmasking the Powers: The Invisible Forces That Determine Human Existence.* Philadelphia: Fortress, 1986.

Worship the Lord: The Liturgy of the Reformed Church in America. New York: Reformed Church Press, 2005.